NEPAL
Nostalgia and Modernity

edited by Deepak Shimkhada

The publication of this book has been made
possible by support received from
Leonardo Vigorelli, Dalton Somaré Gallery, Milan,
and Ahujasons Shawl Wale (P) Ltd., New Delhi

General Editor
PRATAPADITYA PAL

Senior Executive Editor
SAVITA CHANDIRAMANI
Senior Editorial Executive
ARNAVAZ K. BHANSALI
Editorial Executive
RAHUL D'SOUZA

Text Editor
RIVKA ISRAEL

Designer
NAJU HIRANI
Senior Production Executive
GAUTAM V. JADHAV
Production Executive
VIDYADHAR R. SAWANT

Vol. 63 No. 1
September 2011
Price: ₹ 2800.00 / US$ 68.00
ISBN: 978-93-80581-08-8
Library of Congress Catalog Card Number: 2011-312020

Published by Radhika Sabavala for The Marg Foundation at
Army & Navy Building (3rd Floor), 148, M.G. Road, Mumbai 400 001,
India.
Printed at Silverpoint Press Pvt. Ltd., Navi Mumbai
and Processed at The Marg Foundation, Mumbai.

Captions to preliminary pages:
Page 1: A Nepali woman works on a potter's wheel. Photograph:
© Dinodia.
Pages 2–3: Women selling garlands and flowers in front of Kasthamandap
temple at Maru Tole, Hanuman Dhoka Durbar world heritage monument
zone. Photograph: © Dinodia.
Pages 4–5: View of the temple of Pashupatinath in Kathmandu.
Photograph: © Dinodia.
Pages 6–7: Potters' Square, Bhaktapur, Kathmandu Valley. Photograph:
© Dinodia; (inset) Bhairava mask worn by Ashtamatrika dancers of Patan.
Photograph: Caroline Martin.

**Marg's quarterly publications receive support from
the Sir Dorabji Tata Trust – Endowment Fund**

Contents

INTROD

U C T I O N

Deepak Shimkhada

When the real is no longer what it used to be, nostalgia assumes its full meaning.

– Jean Baudrillard

I

In 2007 when Marg invited me to guest edit a volume titled *Nepal: Nostalgia and Modernity*,[1] I immediately jumped at the opportunity even though my plate was full. I was already editing another book and knew firsthand the challenges an editor faces in dealing with a diverse group of contributors from several continents. I soon realized that my academic gluttony was a mistake. But it was too late to back out.

The title grabbed me because the book was about Nepal, a subject dear to my heart. In a sense, my editing of *Nepal: Nostalgia and Modernity* represents a desire to reconnect my present to my past. When I first heard this working title, I was immediately transported to my childhood in Kathmandu, and was able to reconnect emotionally to Nepal, even though I live thousands of miles away in the United States. Because I have lived most of my life outside Nepal, I sometimes feel that I am more of an outsider than an insider. However, unlike memory from a computer chip, childhood memories are so ingrained that they cannot be deleted.

I had to admit that I owed something to Nepal. I had left the country some 39 years ago in the prime of my youth and never returned after I finished my studies in the States. I did not realize that I was attached to Nepal at an unconscious level. Making the decision to not return to Nepal was like a desertion of the country in which I was born, and that decision came to haunt me as I grew older. It produced highly charged emotions I was unable to dislodge from my psyche. The decision to work on this volume was thus like the return of a prodigal son, a payback for this wilful desertion. As redemption for my seemingly sinful act, I wanted to edit the Nepal volume at any cost, so I moved ahead in compiling a list of potential themes and contributors. In the end, I have to admit that the journey was extremely rewarding, albeit fraught with difficulties along the way.

What we have here is a portrait of modern Nepal with its connection to the past, revealed through 11 articles by experts in the field. This new Nepal, poised to enter into the next phase in its history, is not the Nepal I left four decades ago. Within that span of time many things have occurred, including the overthrow of a dynasty that ruled the country for 240 years, and changes in the physical environment, culture, and even religion. The picture presented in this volume is therefore quite striking, unlike any that has been seen before.

1 (previous pages) In the autumn, the Kathmandu Valley usually remains veiled by the morning mist. Photograph: Neetu Wagley.

II

When we speak of the culture of Nepal, we refer to a tiny area of the Kathmandu Valley (figure 1), rich in art and culture. This tiny valley was and still is the heart of Nepal, encompassing 2,000 years of history. Since the time of the Malla kings (c. 1200–1769), the Kathmandu Valley has been essentially urban, with its three major cities of Kantipur, Lalitpur, and Bhadgaon (Kathmandu, Patan, and Bhaktapur). But it is surrounded in large part by a rural setting whose artistic expressions were moulded by agriculture (figure 2). Crops and vegetables grow in the fields throughout the year, managed by *guthi*s (guilds of farmers and artisans). Dotted with water tanks, and with temples and shrines, these verdant fields also serve as community centres for people to come together in building their identity. However, this is changing today in the name of modernization. Where farmers once grew crops and vegetables, suburbs are rapidly expanding, encroaching upon the farmlands.

Although one might think that Kathmandu is hidden away in the slopes of the Himalaya, it has never been totally cut off from the outside world. With open borders, highways, radio and satellite television, and, most importantly, the Internet, Nepal is no longer isolated. Although it lags behind the more advanced nations, modernity has caught up with Nepal, introduced in large part by its citizens wanting changes in politics, social structure, culture, religion, and even art (which is also showing signs of compromise between the past and present). While change signals modernity – moving away from the past – history and nostalgia hold on to the past.

III

Webster's dictionary defines "nostalgia" as the state of being homesick, a wistful, excessively sentimental, or sometimes abnormal yearning for a return to some past period or irrecoverable condition. Further, the etymology of the word reveals that it comes from the Greek *nostos*, meaning to return home, and *aligia*, a painful condition. Combined, "nostalgia" refers to a painful yearning to return home, presumably due to homesickness. Although the term was originally coined by Swiss physician Johannes Hofer[2] in the 17th century to describe the mental condition of Swiss mercenaries while fighting away from home, today nostalgia is not viewed as a disease. Rather, it is a feeling of missing something that is dear to one's life, a yearning to relive or return to one's memories through creative activities. It is thus a longing for often idealized and unrealistic feelings from the past that may or may not be replicated in the present. Because it is associated with fond memories or treasured objects, the emotions can return when a reference to them is made.

Theories abound about nostalgia. Some suggest that nostalgia represents positive feeling toward anything past, no matter how remote or historical.[3] But we live in the present and think in the present, so what causes the triggering of past experience that is loosely understood as nostalgia? If the nostalgic memories are derived from the personally experienced past, does the past cause nostalgia that takes place in the present? Because we are aware of the past (i.e. events that happened in the past), can we not say that the memories of the past are nothing more than the experience of the present? Does this not discount the theory of nostalgia as we hark back for events and memories we left behind? On the contrary, even though the memory of the past takes place in the present, we are still part of the past and we carry those ingrained memories with us like the baggage of a tourist on vacation. While nostalgia refers to the past and modernity to the present, the present cannot be appreciated without the past. In many Western traditions we tend to think of this binary as having two independent entities, ignoring their interconnectedness. However, in Eastern traditions, especially when dealing with

Nepal, the two cannot be separated. A certain amalgamation is found in many artistic expressions of Nepal today, whether traditional or modern, through various agencies that are working together to assert their influence on society and culture. No matter how modern Nepal has become or is on the verge of becoming, its people and culture display features uniquely Nepali in character.

Human beings do not exist in a vacuum, nor can any artist or society. From a Hindu religious point of view it may be explained that what we are today is due to our past actions or deeds in the form of karma. We feed on the past to create the present – and the future makes life whole, since without aspirations, plans, and hopes life is meaningless. However cliched it may sound, there is truth in the statement that without the past we have no present and without the present we have no future. Hindu philosophy finds this

2 Two women preparing the ground for planting vegetables in the Kathmandu Valley. The alluvial soil is soft and easy to turn – ideal for crops. Photograph: Ellie Van Houte.

3 In the morning pigeons gather to collect the rice thrown by worshippers at the Hanuman Dhoka Palace square, Kathmandu. The origins of this palace go back to the time of the Mallas (c. 1200–1768/69). Later it was also used by the kings of the Shah Dynasty, now deposed. In more recent times it has been used only for ceremonial purposes. Photograph: Deepak Shimkhada.

same interdependence within ourselves: the five senses are understood to be as important as the five aggregates – form, feeling, conception, disposition, and consciousness. When we investigate these aspects we realize that they are not isolated elements but related to one another in manifold reverberations of cause and effect, in the same way as karma and samskara.

IV

Artists come and go, but their works remain. This volume focuses on artistic productions in various media and expressions. A variety of artistic and cultural expressions of the Kathmandu Valley are examined by a group of scholars from diverse fields. The confluence of such scholars with different approaches is crucial in bridging the gap previously created by looking at Nepal through a single lens. By highlighting various expressions of art manifested through painting, sculpture, architecture, dance, and even street festivals, the topics of nostalgia and modernity have been juxtaposed to examine the art and culture of Nepal with multiple lenses.

The style of art called Nepali is produced by the Newars, the original inhabitants of the Kathmandu Valley who shaped it from ancient to modern times. The present volume celebrates various artistic expressions of the Newars as well as other ethnic groups that have contributed to the rich artistic and cultural tapestry of the country.

The volume is divided into three parts: (1) Architecture, (2) Visual Arts, and (3) Performances and Religious Traditions. The essays in Part 1 are devoted to Nepal's distinctive architectural expressions in the form of religious monuments such as temples and monasteries, public and private houses including palaces and public squares, and water works such as ghats and public baths. Part 2 has three essays on the visual arts, mainly painting, and one on pottery. Part 3 consists of an array of related subjects: dance, theatre, festivals, and religious practices. The two final essays in this section deal with important aspects of Nepal's two major religions – Hinduism and Buddhism – that have coexisted for centuries. One discusses the Pashupatinath temple, an important shrine of Nepal, where thousands of pilgrims converge on the day of Shivaratri, while the other highlights the virgin cult in the form of Kumari, another syncretic aspect of Nepali religion as couched in Buddhism. Together the four essays in this section provide a wide screen on which to watch the art, culture, and religion of Nepal displayed in their full colours.

V

Building a simple shelter may have been the first attempt of man in the history of human civilization; then came music, dance, painting, sculpture, poetry, and drama in the line of human creativity. The first three essays in this volume are on architecture, both private and public. In the Kathmandu Valley, buildings were traditionally built of baked brick, that gives the city a distinctive appearance, creating a dotted red cityscape. Today, however, with the introduction of concrete and cheaper construction materials, buildings made of baked brick are fast being replaced by perhaps more functional and affordable, but less distinctive and more unattractive, concrete structures (figure 4). Modernism is evident in these buildings that unabashedly display naked iron rods sticking straight up from the second or third storey, obviously making provision

4 A contemporary scene of the Kathmandu Valley with crowded concrete buildings. Photograph: Neetu Wagley.

for future additions. Old and new have thus collided ever since the idea of modernism entered the valley in the 1970s.

An exploration of Nepal's traditional and modern architecture provides a window into how the country has coped with modernity while using traditional forms. The essays here, by three experts from various parts of Europe, explore characteristic aspects of Nepali architecture that are traditional and modern in form. In his essay "Architecture: The Quest for Nepaleseness", Niels Gutschow describes the contributions made by the Newars. He argues that it is the Newars who gave their art "Nepaleseness", a vernacular displayed through brick and woodwork (figure 3).

The adoption of European forms in modern Nepali architecture first appeared in palaces and later in residential buildings. Fanciful forms of Renaissance and Baroque style decorated the majority of buildings in the 20th century after the devastating earthquake of 1934, when a great rebuilding effort was launched that provided an opportunity to jump on the bandwagon of modernity. In her essay titled "In Pursuit of Modernity: The Revival of Classicism in Nepali Architecture", Katharina Weiler traces foreign influences, especially those coming from Europe, on the architecture of the rich and famous. She contends that during the 19th century architectural design based on European ideals spread throughout the world, a movement that arose from the desire to present one uniform style that was not only classical in appearance but also grand and elevating in principle. Nepal, especially Kathmandu, the capital of the country, was no exception. The integration of European style was a way of expressing grandeur, power, and wealth, and this desire is reflected in many buildings constructed by members of the ruling house of Nepal.

In her essay "Living Traditions: Aquatic Architecture and Imagery in the Kathmandu Valley", Julia Hegewald demonstrates that water structures in the Kathmandu Valley are among the most beautiful and striking architectural features of the Himalayan kingdom of Nepal, yet are among the most overlooked and neglected monuments of the region. There appears to be a clear nostalgia for these forms today, since architects are appropriating them in their designs for public buildings such as hotels and civic monuments.

The next three essays present a kaleidoscopic view of Nepali painting from traditional to modern. While Dina Bangdel traces the history of modernism in Nepal from Lain Singh Bangdel, the father of modern painting, to well-recognized but little-known artists in Nepal like Laxman Shreshtha and Jyoti Duwadi, respectively, Ian Alsop examines how modern tourism has influenced the production of paintings known as *paubha*. The history of religious painting in Nepal for both Hindus and Buddhists is ancient. In the past, painters depended on local and Tibetan patrons; today, however, a number of studios in Kathmandu are specializing in traditional *paubha*/thangka paintings by young Nepali artists trained in the old style with the aim of marketing the art to tourists. One could argue that

the interest in ancient art is a revival of tradition. However, the intent is no longer religious but is fuelled primarily by economics, a form of co-modification. In his article, Alsop discusses the religious paintings, primarily Buddhist, which according to him have been produced continuously for more than a thousand years. However, over the last century, traditional religious artists have developed several new schools that have taken the painting of Buddhist and Hindu icons in various new and interesting directions.

Writing about works inspired by tantric forms, Katherine Anne Harper attributes new art for a new age to encroaching secularization, brought on by external influences and internal social change from the mid-20th century. Nepali artists' roles and the art they produce have been revised in response to this changing world. In "Re-Imagining the Universe: Neo-Tantra in Nepal", Harper examines the works of 12 contemporary artists who have used ritual symbols in contemporary, transnational ways.

Whereas paintings and sculptures are displayed in temples, monasteries, homes, and palaces, pottery is part of the people's everyday life. Yet it has received little recognition from scholars as an important art form in Nepal. As demonstrated by the following essay, the art of pottery is an ancient tradition in the Valley and continues to flourish there. Ani Kasten narrates the story of Thimi, located approximately 11 kilometres outside Kathmandu, which is one of the oldest and most important pottery-making centres of Nepal. It is still home to around 10,000 potters, whose families have been working there for centuries according to their caste tradition. While wandering through the narrow alleys of old Thimi, Kasten was struck by the extent to which the village has been preserved as a pottery-producing centre. The tiny alleys paved with brick meander through courtyards filled with villagers conducting all manner of pottery processes, from forming the pots with a wooden paddle to drying them and firing them in traditional straw kilns.

It would not be an exaggeration to say that the three cities of the Kathmandu Valley have fewer streets than alleys. From an alley one emerges into a street where shops are located and the bustle of the city is seen and felt (figure 5). Through the streets, drawn carts and now of course bicycles, autorickshaws, and automobiles compete for space. It is also in the streets where theatre is performed, which forms an important part of the Newar culture in Kathmandu. Dramas based on religious subjects are routinely staged during festivals. Today plays on religious subjects are disappearing from the Kathmandu scene; they are being replaced by theatre of a secular nature. In part 3, the first essay by Sangita Rayamajhi takes the readers through the streets of Harigaon and Kathmandu to witness the *jatras*, the street festivals and plays. *Jatra*s are an integral part of the culture of the Kathmandu Valley that involve practically everyone, either through participation or as audience. It is often said that Newars spend more time celebrating festivals than

5 A street scene in Kathmandu. Photograph: Anders Jenbo.

working. As the carts carrying deities are dragged through the streets, revelry and merrymaking take place with much fanfare, giving rise to Bacchanalian behaviour among the drunken participants, much as in the Mardi Gras. It is also during street festivals such as Gai Jatra, Indra Jatra, or Bisket Jatra that dances and plays are staged in the streets with performers dressed in divine and demonic costumes and masks, much as people dress up for Halloween in America.

These dances and plays are to be seen by everyone in the street (figure 6).[4] However, the tantric religious dance is for the eyes of initiates only, within the confines of a monastery or temple. However, as times have changed so has the tantric dance called Charya Nritya. In her article Miranda Shaw writes, "Many sacred art traditions have been brought to the brink of extinction by social and economic erosions of the priestly role, the rise of anti-religious political movements, the ease of mechanical reproduction, and pressures on local traditions to 'globalize or perish'." The Charya dance tradition of Nepal is no exception. One imperilled sacred art that is bridging the transition to modernity through new channels of transmission and performance is the tantric dance of the Buddhist priests of Nepal, which has now moved out of the Buddhist monasteries

6 *Tamasha* (street show) in Basantpur Square, popularly known as Durbar Square, Kathmandu. Photograph: Rabi Sharma.

and temples to Western stages and classrooms, as Shaw demonstrates in her chapter.

Our book would not be complete without a discussion of religion, because this concerns the faith and beliefs of the people; an investigation allows the reader to understand the country and its people by delving into its roots. The two papers by Tim Ward and myself do just that. In the article "Celebrating Shiva at Pashupati", Tim Ward sits down to chat with a number of naked yogis and semi-clothed babas at Pashupati. In doing so he unfolds the history of the temple. Ward, a Canadian writer who visited Nepal some 15 years ago and wrote about his travels in Nepal and north India in his book *Arousing the Goddess*, returned to Nepal specifically to observe the Shivaratri festival held annually at the temple of Pashupatinath with masses of Hindus attending from all over the country and from India. Writing about Panchla Das, a resident ascetic in Pashupati, Ward states, "For him, the path of a sadhu was a means to get rid of bad karma that he had accumulated in this and past lives. He said his present was devoted to prayer in order to improve his future lives." The Pashupatinath temple has remained a centre of devotion for devout Hindus for centuries and attracts thousands of pilgrims from many parts of India and Nepal, especially sadhus, on the day of Shivaratri. Why sadhus are attracted to Pashupati is a matter of curiosity for Westerners, a question Ward addresses in his article.

In the last piece I deal with the subject of Kumari, the living goddess of Kathmandu. Many sensational articles have recently appeared in the Western media, with titles such as "Kumari in Peril", "Kumari Sacked from Her Throne", "Nepal's Living Goddess Retires", and "Nepal's Living Goddess May Die Soon". The last title may prove to be prophetic because Kumari, as a tradition, is about to become extinct if elements of Nepal's new government and some Western human rights groups have their way. The temple of Kumari, a living embodiment of the Hindu goddess Durga, has been a significant shrine of national importance in Nepal for over three centuries. Ever since Nepal was thrown open to the world with the abolition of the Rana dynasty in the mid-20th century, the temple has also increasingly become a popular tourist attraction. The admixture of politics and religion is not a new phenomenon in the history of Nepal, but for ages the valley has also been an exemplar of Hindu-Buddhist unity. I examine these dynamics that are currently playing roles in determining the fate of Kumari as a living tradition.

VI

With this, the veil that has covered the arts, culture, and religion of Nepal drops, revealing their magnificence and idiosyncrasies. For appreciating the arts, culture, and religion of a nation on a much deeper level, it is necessary to understand its history and the people who produced it. The 11 essays gathered in this volume, I sincerely hope, do just that, with

illustrative examples offering a feast for the eyes. Many books would be required for a full exploration of all things Nepali, but this work focuses on the idea of nostalgia as Nepal moves from the past into modernity and even postmodernity.

The scholars who have contributed to this volume have joined together to offer a vision of how Nepal has changed and how, in many ways, it will remain the same. No country can today remain attached to its past and be oblivious to the forces of modernity. Modernity is everywhere. The Internet fed by satellite has reached the remotest parts of the Himalaya, keeping the people connected with the rest of the world. A young monk walking down the street in a Himalayan landscape with iPod earphones dangling from his ears or speaking on a cell phone or carrying a laptop is not an uncommon sight these days. We have to accept the onset of modernity – whether welcomed by us or forced upon us. I remember a student asking me a question: If the Buddha were to live today, would he use a laptop? The answer is: Absolutely yes – but in moderation. The Buddha would embrace it but not indulge in it to the exclusion of all else. Similarly, in a rich traditional culture such as Nepal's, no attempt to modernize would be successful without embracing the past.

Notes

1 This title was suggested to me by Marg's General Editor, Dr Pratapaditya Pal, at a private meeting at his home in Los Angeles.

2 Johannes Hofer, "Medical Dissertation on Nostalgia", in Carolyn K. Anspach (ed.), *Bulletin of the History of Medicine* 2 (1934), pp. 376–91.

3 Ibid., p. 8.

4 While traditional or modern street plays are performed for entertainment or educational purposes without expectation of any monetary donation, the boy in figure 6 makes a living by creating his own spectacle (a sort of *tamasha*) in one of the main squares in Kathmandu, using stilts. At the end of the performance, the boy asks for donations from the audience.

Part I
ARCHITECTURE

Architecture
The Quest for Nepaleseness

Niels Gutschow

Speaking of the architecture of Nepal, one inevitably refers to the architecture of the Newars: hundreds of Hindu temples, hundreds of Buddhist monastic quadrangles, thousands of shrines, and thousands of stupas, most of them found in the urban setting of the Kathmandu Valley. Till recently, the urban fabric was based on three-storeyed houses built of brick and covered with tiled roofs. Until the 1990s it was considered politically correct to talk of "Nepalese" architecture but since the country is no more a "Hindu kingdom" and aims at a federal republic since early 2008, the ethnic communities within the confines of a country with borders dictated by the colonial power are more than ever in search of their identity. Most of these communities like the Tharu, Rai, Limbu, Thakali, or Magar have developed a distinct village architecture with shrines tied to trees, rocks, and springs. It was only the Newars who developed a rich urban culture based in the Kathmandu Valley, which until recently was identified with "Nepal" by those communities living beyond the confines of that small valley. The Shah kings imported Newar architecture when they or their governors established their palaces at provincial centres from the end of the 18th century. Likewise the Newars themselves took their building habits with them when they migrated to establish trading posts in remote districts.

Numbering no more than half a million people in a country with a population of 26 million, the Newars constitute a minority that used to dominate trade, crafts, and arts. Their origin remains obscure but the Tibeto-Burman language points to Central Asia. The architecture, of which the earliest fragments in stone and wood date to the 6th–8th centuries, borrowed details from the north Indian Kushanas and Guptas[1] but later remained widely untouched by Islamic influences. Motifs such as the baluster column and even the acanthus leaf made their way into Nepal only at the end of the 18th century. At that time also, domed temples and palaces introduced a radically new style fashioned after prototypes from Lucknow and Calcutta (Kolkata) which in turn mirrored English or French ideals. In response, the Newars modernized their domestic architecture by changing the frames and size of windows[2] and introduced pilasters with Corinthian capitals either moulded in mud plaster or cutting bricks to the desired form (see figure 4 in Katharina Weiler, page 32). A consistent craftsmanship in brickmaking and woodcarving keeps ensuring a certain continuity of aesthetic values, on which the recent nostalgia is based.

Continuity and Discontinuity: A Search for Nepaleseness

Since the early 19th century, the Shah dynasty and, as the de facto rulers, the Rana nobility imitated British and Mughal building designs in plaster in a quest to be part of the greater world. A decisive turn took place after the devastating earthquake in 1934. Aiming at a certain independence from British control, Prime Minister Juddha Shumsher Rana decided to build a prestigious structure in neoclassical style in the centre of Kathmandu, complete with pediment and columns into which large decorative Newar-style windows were incorporated. While the adjoining shop-fronts were standardized and decidedly modern, the Sabha Griha[3] obviously was meant to demonstrate a certain Nepaleseness and this resulted in the invention of carved window elements, albeit in new scale and even on ground-floor level. Obviously, Juddha Shumsher wanted to be "modern" but at the same time he wanted to tie himself to the location and that needed some kind of Newarization. This move can not at all be qualified as nostalgic but as a political statement and a gesture of reconciliation or even appeasement.

With the return of the Shah dynasty to power, the 1950s witnessed administrational and economic modernization, but Nepaleseness was needed when it came to ritual. When King Mahendra was crowned in 1956, the coronation platform (mandapa) was covered with tiered roofs, of which the coronation book mentioned: "It looks just like a pagoda. This indicates that the Royal Sovereigns are the objects of worship next to God."[4] When Mahendra's son Birendra was crowned in 1975, a similar but much more elaborate platform was constructed, later dismantled and translocated to the Botanical

Garden in Godavari where it still stands today (figure 1). The structure defies all proportional considerations but with carved panels and a two-tiered roof in copper sheet it represents an ultimate Nepaleseness and sets standards for the coming decades.

The image of the pyramidal roof – originally reserved for temples – had entered domestic architecture[5] already in the 1970s. Suddenly the third storey of box-like structures needed such a cap of corrugated iron sheets, while flat roofs demonstrated contemporary values of modernity. Not unimportant in this context was the return of brick as face material which was propagated by the Austrian architect Carl Pruscha with the construction of his own house in 1969 and the Taragaon Hotel complex with its conspicuous vaults in brick. The restoration of the Pujari Math in Bhaktapur[6] in 1971 and subsequently the activities of the Bhaktapur Development Project (1974–86) added to this notion with the revival of the veneer brick (Nepali *telia ita*, Newari *dachiapa*) and moulded cornice bricks, which until the mid-1990s were individually

1 Platform (mandapa), built in 1975 on Tundhikhel Square (the maidan) in Kathmandu on the occasion of the coronation of King Birendra Bir Bikram Shah, later dismantled and re-erected at the Botanical Garden in Godavari. The tiered roofs with finial and carved wooden panels covering a reinforced concrete structure stand for a Nepaleseness that has no historical precedent. The platform does not represent a replica but the vague imitation of tradition that leads to new forms.

moulded, carved by hand, and fired by traditional brickmakers of the community of Avale. With the casting of moulds by foundries in Bihar the scene changed fundamentally. Prices were cut by half, making such bricks available for a wide range of building projects. Earlier, such bricks were used almost exclusively for projects of architectural heritage preservation or ambitious reconstructions like the Chyasilin Mandapa (1987–90) on Bhaktapur's Durbar Square;[7] by 1995 they decorated the face of shop-fronts like the Bally shoe shop opposite the nine-storeyed Durbar in Kathmandu. The following decade witnessed "Nepalese" veneer bricks replacing "Chinese" bricks from modern brick factories – labelled "Chinese" after the first modern kiln erected with Chinese support in Harisiddhi in the mid-1960s.

The Emergence of Nepalese Style

The urge to demonstrate Nepaleseness with pyramidal roofs became evident in the 1980s at a time when the autocratic panchayat system of King Birendra came under pressure.

Official architecture had to be neither modern, nor Indian, but Nepalese. Robert Weise, the first foreign architect from Switzerland who practised in Nepal since 1959, set an early standard in the 1970s with pyramidal roofs for the Hotel Yellow Pagoda at Jamal, the Civil Aviation building next to Baber Mahal, and a number of barracks for the army. In the mid-1980s the government followed an aggressive path in an urge to demonstrate Nepaleseness. The Bahadur Bhawan, built in 1889 by Bir Shumsher, was converted into the Hotel Royal as the country's first tourist hotel, returned to the government in 1970, and 15 years later Newarized. The roof pavilions in the shape of Rajasthani chhattris or Bangla roofs were dismantled and replaced by tiered pagoda structures. Likewise, the Vivaha Mandapa (the marriage platform of Ram and Sita) at the Janaki Temple in Janakpur, established in 1899 by the Queen of Orchha, was incorporated into a new two-tiered pagoda, designed by Uttam Krishna Shrestha from the Department of Housing in 1983. With glass panels in aluminium frames, the temple achieved a certain modernity, unlike the pillared

2 (above) and 3 (overleaf) Royal Nepal Academy in Kathmandu. Designed by Shankar Nath Rimal in 1968 as a "modern" structure with a dynamic roofline, the building was Newarized in the mid-1980s by an arcaded, roofed entrance and a gate flanked by pavilions roofed with gilded copper sheet.

4 Transformation of the Durbar Square, Bhaktapur, in response to the filmmaker Bernardo Bertolucci's vision of an urban space that aims beyond historical evidence. The square's space was reduced, a new gate invented, and the square equipped with a platform framed by elephants and palm trees. The palace, originally white, was painted red, and received a two-storeyed arcade crafted in foam.

"Nepalese Pagoda" built in the same year in Munich on the occasion of the International Garden Exhibition. Common to all these structures are squat proportions alien to temples of the Malla period (14th–18th centuries).

Even more significant was the transformation of the Royal Nepal Academy in 1985 (figures 2 and 3). Designed in 1968 by Shankar Nath Rimal, Nepal's first engineer who named his firm "Engineers & Architects" after he returned from his studies at the Bengal Engineering College in Calcutta, the building was basically a floating white box projecting across the ground floor with Newar-style windows and a dynamic roof covering the central audience hall. Obviously, at one point the National Academy had to be more Nepalese. For that purpose a glazed hall, daringly projecting above the entrance, was incorporated into a temple-like structure in 1985, with a Newarized arcade below and a roof complete with a finial on top. To add to this new identification of a new building type in a nondescript modern style with Nepal, the gateway received two pillars, flanked by square pavilions. All of these

elements were equipped with sloped metal roofs and finials to arouse associations with the idea of the pagoda, located in the imagined landscape of Shangri-La.

Ironically, this fantasy was further elaborated by the filmmaker Bernardo Bertolucci, who chose Bhaktapur as the stage for the film *Little Buddha* in October–November 1992. The palace square was too large to serve his purpose and the main structure of the former palace had unfortunately been refashioned by Dhir Shumsher Rana in 1855 to accommodate a large audience hall, complete with an English-style fireplace. As the Lucknow-style face of the palace in white plaster did not fulfil the filmmaker's expectations, he had it painted red, while a two-storeyed arcade (figure 4) was added within days to create the nondescript Nepaleseness of the urban environment – made for the Buddha.

The "Bittersweet Longing" of Nostalgia
The American Heritage Dictionary tells us that nostalgia is characterized by "a bittersweet longing". In architecture,

5 and 6 Infill within the World Heritage Site of Patan, implementing design standards postulated by the municipality and the Department of Archaeology. Squeezed in between houses from the early 1940s and '80s, the bearing structure in reinforced concrete receives a face of veneer bricks and dividing cornices to recall a "traditional" character. The early-19th-century triple window at second-floor level has been salvaged from the earlier demolished house.

the bittersweetness manifests itself in a variety of forms. The dream of the Bhaktapur Development Project's planners, manifested in its by-laws stipulated since the late 1970s, finally materialized with the emergence of strong municipalities with democratic legitimacy in the mid-1990s. Since then house-owners are forced to use veneer bricks for the building's front face, and moulded bricks for the cornice and upright window proportions. In terms of architecture, the Newarization became mere decoration, as the bearing system is inevitably a reinforced concrete structure (figures 5 and 6). As soon as steel rods from India and cement imported from Indonesia were no more traded on the black market but became available in large quantities at affordable prices in the early 1980s, new interior spaces with high ceilings became common not only for free-standing houses as the fulfilment of the ultimate dream of the upper middle class, but also for infill structures within the historic core areas. In Bhaktapur, the municipality even offered the veener bricks and a certain quantity of wood for the window-frames free of charge for projects within the entire historic core, as long as the owner complied with the municipality's design requirements. Quite a few brick factories keep a wide range of moulded bricks in stock and advertise their products with the motto "A Touch of History" (figure 7). To avoid trouble in the process of obtaining a permit, owners just ask the overseers of the municipalities to design their house. Rare cases – like the house at Patan's Durbar Square designed by Dinesh Amatya in 1998 (figure 8) – are carefully

8 House of Maitri Shakya (Dharmachakra Art Traders) at the palace square, Patan, designed by Dinesh Amatya in 1998. With increased ceiling heights, the house changes the traditional scale, while the sloped roof with its dormer, the cornices, the newly carved projecting triple window with latticed shutters, and the panelled door leaves create a somewhat vague sense of continuity.

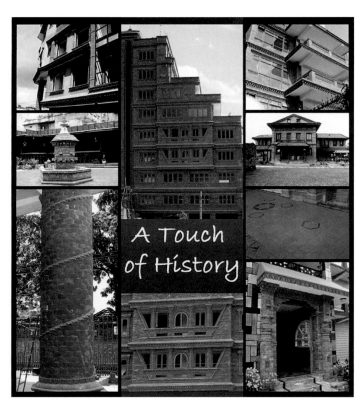

7 Advertisement from a magazine of the Shree Dakshin Barahi Brick Factory, demonstrating nine examples of using moulded bricks to achieve "A Touch of History".

designed by architects trained abroad, usually in the Soviet Union or India.

As the next article by Katharina Weiler demonstrates, at present architects and their clients may choose among (1) a postmodern house which reflects design standards advertised by international magazines, (2) a house with neoclassical elements reflecting the arrival of Punjabi Baroque,[8] or (3) a Newarized house with tiled roofs and a mixture of newly carved windows and fragments salvaged from dismantled houses. The house of Jayaram Acharya, designed by Surya Bhakta Sangachhe, perfectly documents the third option. It is described as an "adaptation of traditional elements to modern sensibilities"[9] (figure 9) and stands for the dream of the upper middle class to identify with local traditions. Born in 1950 in Bhaktapur and trained in the School of Architecture in Kiev, Sangachhe became Acting Director General of the Department of Urban Development in 2008 and introduced a completely new design to Kathmandu's buildings, conflating the syntax of the local architectural language in a postmodern era. Borrowing the idea of the villa from the Britishers and the Ranas, the house displays a touch of Nepaleseness that demonstrates self-confidence and probably an awareness of the necessity for preserving traditions of a unique architectural heritage. Windows salvaged from demolition sites are freely mixed with newly carved ones.

The Tourist Perspective

Overriding the notion of nostalgia's bitterness, the presentation of its sweetness would be incomplete without recent hotel projects. The Hotel Meridien, for example, designed by Romi Khosla from Delhi and completed in 2005 within the large compound of a golf course, introduces a variety of design elements which turn the place into something modern yet with an echo of tradition. Lime-coated cottages have sturdy

brick pillars, capitals, and lintels in steel (figures 10 and 11). While the bearing profiles are camouflaged by wooden planks, the capital is carefully designed in steel to mirror 17th-century prototypes. Khosla roughly based this design on the Patan Museum, developed by Götz Hagmüller in the early 1990s.[10]

Much larger and bulkier, the Hyatt hotel at Bodhnath (figure 12) turns out to be a rather rough version of the tourist's dream of arriving in Nepal. Large tiled roofs and tiered towers flanking the entrance to the lobby are overdone in scale, but the lobby itself offers place for nine Buddhist votive structures (stupas, called chaityas in the Nepalese context) which were crafted by local stonecarvers from the Shakya community (figure 13). All of these not only represent faithful (or even "authentic") replicas of structures found in the urban space of the Newars; the stupas also underwent the entire sequence of Buddhist lifecycle rituals (*dashakarma*) to become powerful

9 Residence of Jayaram Acharya in Sainbu, Lalitpur district, designed by Surya Bhakta Sangachhe in 2005. Photograph: Stanislaw Klimek.

10 and 11 Hotel Meridien Gokarna, designed by Romi Khosla of Delhi in 1995, completed in 2005. The project involved restoration of a typical early-20th-century house to accommodate a suite. The free-standing house in the garden of the hotel compound was re-roofed, the window openings enlarged, and the ground floor opened by a five-bayed colonnade with columns. The columns designed in steel recall the ancient Newar formula of post and beam structure in wood.

12 and 13 (opposite) Hyatt Regency, Kathmandu, designed by Wong Chu Man from Nikken Seiken in 1996 and completed in 2000. In a vague imitation of Newar design elements, the five-star hotel introduces sloped roofs with struts in concrete and decorative window frames. Tiered towers flanking the entrance recall the "pagoda" motif. Designed by Bijay Basukala and Niels Gutschow, nine chaityas – faithful replicas of Buddhist votive architecture found in urban spaces – which dot the spacious court underwent the proper lifecycle rituals to be imbued with "life".

symbols of the Buddha. The parallel world of tourism is absolutely content with replicas in a safe environment. Bitter or sweet – it is a reality which leads us to talk of the "authenticity of the replica" once the craftsmanship is convincing.

Epilogue

We may sum up the formative activities of the 1970s and '80s: (1) international cooperation in the field of preservation of the architectural heritage; (2) the impulse of foreign planners to guide the townscape with by-laws advocating sloped roofs, vertical window proportions, and exposed brickwork; (3) a precarious nation in search of an identity; and (4) the tourism industry propagating a hidden Shangri-La with pagodas, unspoilt mountains, and supposedly innocent and happy people. All this prepared the ground for a sweeping nostalgia in which developers of shopping malls and builders of houses joined.

The most radical dream in pursuit of nostalgia is dreamt by Comrade Narain Man Bijukchen, respected leader of the Bhaktapur-based Nepal Workers' and Peasants' Party. Recently he published a booklet titled "Bhaktapur 100 Years Hence" in which the fictive diary of one Ramu is presented. On December 23, 2099 Ramu opens an old book dated 1999 and reads the following report:

> Nearly a quarter of the houses of Bhaktapur City has been built of cement and concrete. There are many houses made of cement, iron rods and concrete and Nepali bricks and tiles are being pasted on their outer walls just like clothes. Five or six-storeyed houses have been built by violating the standards of the municipality. Black water tanks are seen on the roofs of the houses. The antennas, solar water heating panels, all of these have deformed the upper part of Bhaktapur.

Ramu turns to his diary and writes:

> I was terrified of the description hundred years back. I closed the book and went to the roof. The sun had risen. No, there weren't tall and small roofs, there were only uniform red tiled roofs. There weren't black ugly water tanks, wires of telephone, electricity and television. I was very happy and full of pride – my roofs, balconies and temples are glorious and beautiful as before.

The leader of the local leftist party illustrates his publication with a couple of drawings of the existing townscape and confronts these with his dream – street elevations stripped of any sign of modernity.

In summer 2007 Hisila Yami of the Maoist Party was appointed Minister of Public Works and Planning. She and her husband Baburam Bhattarai – both had studied architecture in India, and met in the early 1980s at Delhi's Jawaharlal Nehru University where he attained a Doctor of Philosophy in 1986 – were the intellectual fountainheads of their party, which gained a third of all the votes in a free election in April 2008. What will their vision be? How will their party mediate between the fictive Nepaleseness of a federal republic and modernity embedded in a globalized economy?

Figure Acknowledgements
All photographs by the author except figures 7 and 9.

Notes
1   See U. Wiesner, *Nepalese Temple Architecture* (Leiden, 1978).
2   See N. Gutschow, "Newar Windows as Elements of Architecture", in J. Pieper and G. Michell (eds.), *The Impulse to Adorn* (Bombay: Marg Publications, 1982), pp. 63–78.
3   Andreas Proksch (ed.), *Images of a Century. The Changing Townscapes of the Kathmandu Valley* (Kathmandu, 1995), p. 72.
4   *The Coronation Book of Their Majesties of Nepal* (Calcutta, c. 1956), p. xxi.
5   G. Auer and N. Gutschow, "Domestic Architecture of Nepal", in *Art and Archaeology Research Papers*, Vol. 12 (December 1977), p. 69.
6   N. Gutschow, "Die Restaurierung des Pujahari Math in Bhaktapur/Nepal", *Deutsche Kunst und Denkmalpflege*, Vol. 30, No. 2 (Munich, 1972), pp. 102–18.
7   N. Gutschow and G. Hagmüller, "The Reconstruction of the Cyasilin Mandap", *Ancient Nepal*, Nos. 123–25 (Kathmandu, 1991), pp. 1–9, reprinted in K.E. Larsen and N. Marstein (eds.), *ICOMOS International Wood Committee (IIWC) 8th International Symposium* (Nepal, 1992), pp. 133–47.
8   Gautam Bhatia, *Punjabi Baroque and Other Memories of Architecture* (New Delhi, 1994).
9   "Nepalese Designer's Building Plans", *Architecture & Interiors*, Vol. 4 (c. 2005), pp. 39–41.
10 Götz Hagmüller, *Patan Museum: The Transformation of a Royal Palace in Nepal* (London, 2003), p. 77.

In Pursuit of Modernity
The Revival of Classicism in Nepali Architecture

Katharina Weiler

During the 19th century architectural design based on European ideals spread throughout the world. This arose from a desire to present one uniform style that was not only classical in appearance but also grand and elevating in principle. Even before the term "globalization" had been coined, the concept occurred on a global scale. Economic power and ambitions for political power drove many rulers in Asia to modernize, making way for the accommodation of a European style of architecture based on classicism. From the first half of the 19th century, non-European rulers in Asia and elsewhere began building Western-style palaces. Initially the Rana rulers of Nepal oriented the design of their palace architecture towards the classical European style; however, although Nepal was not a British colony, Rana palaces did reflect British cultural values, as did some of the palaces built by the maharajas in India. In a sense, these palaces heralded an architectural language that essentially wanted to be modern.

As a result, the Newar architecture of the Kathmandu Valley underwent a radical change in the middle of the 19th century. Neoclassical forms were finally incorporated in numerous residential buildings as well. Alongside neoclassical and local design even Islamic motifs, dating back to the time of Mughal rule in northern India, were chosen as decor and were intermingled in a hybrid Newar building style. The most important cities that demonstrated this new style in the Kathmandu Valley were the ancient cities of Kathmandu, Patan, and Bhaktapur, in which the new language of architecture characterized the townscape. Plastered and decorated with stucco, the houses built in the first half of the 20th century – the majority of them after a devastating earthquake in 1934 – replaced the red-toned brick facades and today still give the cities of Kathmandu and Patan their genius loci.

Imitating Neoclassical Design

Classical architecture in Asia was often critically discussed in Europe during the 19th century. The arguments denounced an architectural style considered to be eclectic. Visitors from Europe regarded the buildings in Kathmandu as imitations that lacked the principles of their structural elements. They were said to bear no reference to their environment. The Europeans, however, never compared Nepali affection for European styles with the Western love of Asian forms. The Baroque and Palladian style appealed to the Ranas and Newars in Nepal in a manner similar to the way Eastern art traditions were transformed into Chinoiserie and Indian Gothic by Europeans, evoking in the spectator a sense of the exotic. These architectural exchanges expressed cultural flows in both directions, engendering a meeting of East and West and its transcultural outcome.

In the Kathmandu Valley, where neoclassical palaces had been built and European forms incorporated into the residential architecture by the Newars, such forms only resemble European design. The early-20th-century architecture of the Kathmandu Valley reflects various ways of copying associated with the arrival of European architecture in Nepal and its interaction with local forms. The architecture provides an imitation of European buildings,

1 Post-earthquake "New Road" in Kathmandu: modern houses with neoclassical features formed the elegant broad boulevard, erected under Juddha Shumsher in 1934. In the early 21st century, neoclassicism is seeing a renaissance in Nepal, though the proportions have been changing and the acanthus capitals intermingle with mirror glass.

modification of indigenous forms, and the constitution of new styles. The edifices are neither wholly Nepali nor truly European – they are buildings of hybrid principles creating a new architectural vocabulary of their own. What were the causes of such an adaptation of European neoclassical vocabulary for use in Nepali architecture?

The Rana Palaces: European Citations as Representational Architecture

The Ranas, who came to power in Nepal and eventually ruled the country for more than a hundred years, built their palaces in part to reflect the grandeur of the British Raj. The West was perceived as the seat of imperialism and the source of modernization, and palace architecture became a vehicle through which Western power could be displayed and communicated to Nepali citizens. With Jung Bahadur Rana, especially after his historic visit to Europe in 1850, modernity took its roots in the process of Europeanization in Nepal. Thapathali, the prime minister's residence, was a whitewashed palace with stucco decor in the grand neoclassical style that appealed to Jung Bahadur during his travels to Great Britain and France in the middle of the 19th century. It was a trendsetter in demonstrating a completely new lifestyle at the Rana's court, that was kept alive for the following hundred years of Rana rule. With grand palaces, columns, neoclassical porticos, rococo public rooms, Italian Carrara marble, ornate furniture reflecting Victorian taste, European and Oriental bric-a-brac, and, last but not least, cars, the Rana rulers lived in the lap of European luxury at all times. The portraits of Jung Bahadur next to those of Queen Victoria and Prince Albert in the halls of Thapathali illustrate the wish to be coevals and partners in global politics.

The introduction of modern technologies, infrastructure, and social reforms in Nepal is attributed to Chandra Shumsher Rana (1901–24). Of all the palaces built under the Ranas, none surpassed the Singha Durbar (1903), built by Chandra Shumsher, in size and grandeur. It was said to be the largest palace in Asia. The number of these neoclassical palaces – the Kathmandu Valley boasted more than 40 – represents the consistent mass representation of modern power. Europe was equated with consistency, classicism, and noblesse; the European quotation signified the achievement of a materially defined world class. The rulers adapted a European lifestyle of which architecture was probably the most representative feature.

The Ranas' adaptation of a European architectural language and lifestyle considered as modern can be regarded as "breaking with tradition", the caesura in the language of well-known Nepali techniques and patterns. In the Newar residences neoclassical forms interacted with local design. In the first half of the 20th century neoclassicism was "contemporary" and characteristic of the Nepali present. Whereas in Europe classicism had to be equated with tradition and nostalgia – a sentimental yearning for the past – in Nepal it stood for projection into the future.

Rebuilding after the Earthquake

The Kathmandu Valley has been subjected to minor and major earthquakes in modern times. The most devastating one in recent memory struck the valley in January 1934, levelling and damaging a large number of buildings – homes, palaces, and even temples. In the months and years that followed, an overall urban rebuilding took place under Prime Minister Juddha Shumsher Rana. He was the builder of the post-earthquake "New Road" in Kathmandu, an elegant, broad boulevard with eclectic neoclassical architecture for the newly styled city (figure 1). As elsewhere in the city core, impressive noblemen's houses with plastered facades and aspiring columns lined the street giving a new face to the formerly old and narrow focus.

Houses with European features had already been erected in the first decades of the 20th century. The great rebuilding after the earthquake, however, was taken as an opportunity by the Newar population to extensively jump on the bandwagon of modernity. The dimension of modern housing after 1934 points out the different trends in the cities of Bhaktapur, Kathmandu, and Patan. In Kathmandu and Patan people favoured fully and partially plastered facades. Stucco decor testifies to sophisticated workmanship. In Bhaktapur the houses remained primarily unrendered, and rustic interpretations of neoclassical forms were expressed in brick. The most striking aspect concerning residential buildings is the fact that modernization happened on the surface, the facade. The rest of the house was arranged as it had been for generations, due to the functional organization and symbolic order of the Newar house. Thus tradition in the Newar context was not the opposite of modernity. Today this becomes especially obvious in Bhaktapur's newly built houses, where building techniques with brick and wood are being reinvented in order to present a certain "Nepaleseness" (see article by Niels Gutschow).

Newar Modernity

Fanciful forms of Renaissance and Baroque style decorated the majority of buildings of the 20th-century settlements in the Kathmandu Valley before and after 1934. The Newar sculptors found the models for their design repertoire in the neoclassical Rana architecture and European pattern books. Although the decorations are designed individually from house to house, an interrelation of key elements can be verified. There is harmony concerning the houses' heights, the number of three or four floors, and the construction techniques. Inherently European forms were admitted as novelties in the Nepali architecture, such as the plastered facade, segment gables, balustrades, and pilasters framing the facades (figure 2). There are similarities in the nature of certain neoclassical stucco ornaments, like

flowering cartouches with inscriptions as well as meander and metope-triglyph friezes. Lions and heavenly female figures in European style adorn many facades (figure 3). A change in proportions was undertaken in the format and position of windows. The vertical window opening that became generally accepted replaced the horizontal Newar lattice window. The avoidance of strict vertical and horizontal alignment of windows in the buildings of Malla times was widely replaced by the Western neoclassical method of positioning them accurately one above another. What prima facie resemble cast-iron balustrades in the residential facades emerge on closer inspection as perfectly imitated woodcarvings in the manner of European patterns.

What became modern for the Newars was geared not only to certain principles of the European classic and historified neoclassical forms or just European designs. There is not a total disregard of local forms, but rather an inexplicable "Newarness" in the facades owing to the builder's cultural, social, and religious environment (figure 4). The houses reflect

2 Asan Tole, Kathmandu: in the first half of the 20th century, impressive noblemen's houses with plastered facades, aspiring Ionic columns, and cast-iron or wooden balustrades resembling European design were built in the city core. They gave a new face to the formerly old and narrow centre.

the multiple identities of the Newar builders and inhabitants that combined both indigenous values and an imported modernity. A jaunty kind of indigenous Nepali modernity characterizes the residences, while still harmonizing with their historic environment.

In the Kathmandu Valley modernity was characterized by the borrowing and blending of new forms with the traditional architectural vocabulary. The next step in the history of modern Nepali architecture is mirrored in the houses' plain, repetitive fronts and flat roofs, affected by the Indian modern style and widely built from the middle of the 1950s. These bungalows and freestanding houses mushroomed at the peripheries of the towns.

3 Amatya house (1945) at Durbar Square, Patan: until the middle of the 20th century, whitewashed facades with neoclassical stucco embellishments testify to the sophisticated workmanship in the Kathmandu Valley. The lion became a popular attachment to modern houses.

4 Piya house (c. 1934), Tulache Tole in Bhaktapur: in Bhaktapur, the houses primarily remained unrendered, and local interpretations of neoclassical forms were expressed in brick.

The Nostalgic View of Rana Architecture

The Rana palaces were nationalized in 1966; many of them house government offices at present. While some Rana palaces are decaying due to lack of maintenance and preservation, others have been converted into hotels. Simultaneously, the neoclassical architecture – once modern in the Rana period and today nostalgically associated with the former glory of Nepal – has been accredited to a cultural heritage in the last decades.

Heritage Hotels

Some former Rana palaces have today been converted into hotels that render homage to bygone glory. The former neoclassical palace of Jit Shumsher Rana, Agni Bhawan (1894), had already been converted into the high-class Hotel Shanker in 1964 (figure 5). The hotel advertises with the slogan "Old World Elegance" and offers the "royal treatment you deserve". The facade was kept more or less intact while the interior was redesigned to give travellers modern comforts. Rana ambience is evident in the Kailash Restaurant and the Durbar Hall, formerly a princely Rana ballroom, with its neoclassical interior design and antique chandeliers.

In the 1970s the Russian Boris Lissanevitch restored a palace wing of Lal Durbar, once the palace of Rudra Shumsher Rana, and established in it a restaurant called "Yak and Yeti". Today the former palace wing is part of the five-star hotel of the same name. It boasts Rana heritage such as the exalted entrance hall with its portraits of the Rana maharajas and maharanis. The "Regency Hall" that was also used by the Ranas is a fully restored hall for public use, adorned with antique mirrors and murals. The "Dynasty Hall" was the private meeting room of the Rana rulers and is still decorated with exquisite antique chandeliers, mirrors, and portraits of the Rana royalty.

Baber Mahal Revisited

Another recent return to Nepali neoclassical heritage is exemplified in the renovation called "Baber Mahal Revisited". In 1913 Rana Prime Minister Maharaja Chandra Shumsher completed the construction of a palace named Baber Mahal for his son Baber Shumsher. Today the stables, cowsheds, and outbuildings of his palace are contemporary concepts based on Rana architecture. They comprise "Baber Mahal Revisited", an exquisitely remodelled shopping compound in which the imitated Rana architecture is blended with Newar design (figure 6).

Gautam S.J.B. Rana, the great-great-grandson of Prime Minister Chandra Shumsher, lived in Baber Mahal until 1966

5 Hotel Shanker, Kathmandu: the former neoclassical palace of Jit Shumsher Rana, Agni Bhawan (1894) was converted into the high-class Hotel Shanker in 1964.

6 Baber Mahal Revisited, Kathmandu: designed by Erich Theophile and Rohit Ranjitkar for Gautam Rana in 1994, and completed in 1997, the project involved the adaptation of former stables within the compound of the Baber Mahal Palace and their re-creation into a shopping complex. Photograph: Stanislaw Klimek.

7 Garden of Dreams, Kathmandu: Keshar Shumsher Rana's garden of c. 1920, with a sophisticated ensemble of pavilions, fountains, pergolas, urns, and statues, is an enduring legacy of the Rana aristocracy. In the late 1990s, the Austrian architect Götz Hagmüller renovated the garden. Photograph: Götz Hagmüller.

when the government nationalized it and moved the offices of the Ministry of Roads there. His family was given the adjacent carriage house and stables. By the 1990s the structures were in disrepair. Gautam Rana wistfully longed for the past and had the idea for the "Revisited" project to be built on his family plot. In 1996 Erich Theophile, an American architect who had been involved in restoring historic architecture in the Kathmandu Valley since 1990, created the design for the remodelling along with the Nepali architect Rohit Ranjitkar. The existing historical buildings and foundations were used, and new building blocks inserted to create a sequence of courtyards and alleys. The design was totally integrated into the old building structure, and was given a new look only by adding pitched roofs. Additionally, antique vertical windows of early-20th-century Newar houses, salvaged from Patan, were reused. At that time, adaptive reuse as at "Baber Mahal Revisited" was still a revolutionary idea in Nepal. There was a nostalgic need to create a pastiche of Rana glory, and marketing the idea of using old buildings required the augmentation of new design without any strong imposition of contemporary style.

The Garden of Dreams

Keshar Shumsher Rana's Garden of Dreams (Swapna Bagaicha) in Kathmandu, built in the 1920s, is a tranquil oasis in the midst of hectic Kathmandu and an enduring legacy of the Rana aristocracy (figure 7). The Nepali engineer Kishwor Narsingh Rana was responsible for the detailed layout and execution of the garden, following the instructions of his distinguished client Keshar Shumsher – a statesman, scholar, linguist, and connoisseur of horticulture, art, and literature. Within this neoclassical garden is found a sophisticated ensemble of pavilions, fountains, decorative garden furniture, pergolas, balustrades, urns, and statues – all based on European models. In the pavilions, dedicated to the six seasons – Basanta (spring), Grishma (summer), Barkha (the monsoon season), Sharad (early autumn), Hemanta (late autumn), and Shishir (winter) – Keshar Shumsher cultivated a wide variety of local and exotic plants.

After the Rana rule ended the garden fell into neglect and decay. The stately garden paths were overgrown by weeds. The garden area was originally twice as large, but members of

8 Mansion in Sanepa, Patan (2001): behind high gates, neoclassical forms are reused in the 21st century as distinctive features of wealthy homes. Porticos or acanthus capitals, both substitutes for globally accepted European classic design and today nostalgically associated with the former glory of Nepal, are found at private residences as well as banks and restaurants, cinemas and shopping malls. Photograph: Stanislaw Klimek.

the family sold off a section to developers. Lok Bhakta Rana and his mother donated the remaining 0.6-hectare section to the Nepali government in the mid-1960s. The government, however, allowed the garden to fall into disrepair – the western part was lost due to the urban expansion of the tourist quarter Thamel where three pavilions were demolished.

In the late 1990s the Austrian architect Götz Hagmüller, renowned for his restoration work at the World Heritage Site of Bhaktapur and his restoration of the Patan Museum, made the effort to renovate the garden. The garden has been reactivated with the support of Austrian Development Aid and in collaboration with the Ministry of Education, then HMG Nepal, and executed by the Austrian non-profit organization Eco Himal. A number of elements were added, that utilized latent vestiges of its existing layout and architecture. An amphitheatre was created for cultural programmes, and two of the historical pavilions were converted: in 2007 the Barkha pavilion in the southwestern corner of the compound was transformed into a Viennese lounge bar designed by Götz Hagmüller, and the Basanta pavilion was turned into a tea salon run by the Dwarika Hotel. The rotunda was reconstructed as a new focal point along with new fountains and pergolas. Statues of white elephants and wooden benches in the Art Deco style were reconstructed by utilizing historic photographs. As a cultural heritage landmark of Kathmandu, the garden is destined to be an attraction for locals and tourists, who are given the opportunity to walk in the footsteps of the Rana who built it, and experience the builder's elegant lifestyle.

The Renaissance of Classicism

From the beginning of the 21st century, the Indian-style bungalows that set the trend for residential buildings after Rana rule have again been continuously superseded in Nepal by a revival of neoclassical architectural forms. Upper-class villas in the Kathmandu Valley are built in a similar north Indian style known as "Punjabi Baroque". Neoclassical styles have also been chosen for the modern urban architecture and gated communities of the new rich in the cities of Bangkok, Delhi, Kiev, Manila, Beijing, and elsewhere. In this Nepali renaissance of classicism, European forms are used from the global construction kit of the wealthy. The tympanum and classical orders behind high walls are distinctive signs of Nepali bourgeois living standards, as well as a representative gate and guard to watch the compound. In Nepal, the portico and the acanthus capital, both substitutes for globally accepted European classical design, are found in private residences as well as banks, restaurants, cinemas, and shopping malls (figure 8). During Rana rule the colonnades of the palaces were characterized by white shafts and black capitals. As a relic from the past, the new capitals of today are often painted black. The proportions have been changing, and the columns aspire synchronically to the heights of buildings. Pilasters of early-20th-century houses frame the facade in each storey, or

9 Changing faces of modernity: a shop window in Patan mirrors a plain and repetitive facade, once modern in the 1980s, while exhibiting classical interior decoration in styrofoam. In contrast, neoclassical design was modelled individually in stucco plaster during the first half of the 20th century.

span the first and second floors. Today the abandonment of the symbolic order of the Newar house and the loss of the definite number of three floors allow the design of columns of a truly colossal order, extending across three or more storeys. These underline the vertical extension of Newar cities.

Epilogue

Modernity can be understood as the awareness of the newest developments, a process of borrowing and assimilation. From the middle of the 19th until the middle of the 20th century, a blend of neoclassical and indigenous forms characterized Nepali modern architecture. The Newars built architectural responses to the Rana palaces that had in turn been inspired by the colonial architecture in India. Today Nepali neoclassicism is referred to as cultural heritage, while nostalgia with a reference to Nepali history is evident. Coevally, there are classical forms produced as goods in bulk that contrast and, at the same time, intermingle with contemporary modern mirror glass and cement (figure 9). In this case the classical forms are again considered modern as Nepal once more follows an Asian trend.

Figure Acknowledgements
All photographs by the author except figures 6–8.

Living Traditions
Aquatic Architecture and Imagery in the Kathmandu Valley

Julia A.B. Hegewald

Situated on the banks of rivers and the edges of the Himalayan foothills, the three royal foundations – Kathmandu, Patan, and Bhaktapur – are rich in water.[1] Over the centuries, a series of architectural features were developed to make the water of the rivers safely accessible, at often considerably changing levels, and to utilize the secured embankments for the performance of rituals. Groundwater is retrieved from great depth through wells, and shallow aquifers are tapped and made to issue through spouts and fountains, providing fresh drinking water. Surplus water from these conduit fountains and rainwater are stored in large reservoirs for bathing and watering animals.

Water architecture in the Kathmandu Valley constitutes complex engineering achievements and great accomplishments in water management. Water structures are also places where sacred statues are enshrined and venerated, and where water-related rituals are conducted. This indicates the multifaceted functions of many of the elaborate water sites spread throughout the valley. Despite the introduction of modern technology, a large number of traditional water structures are still in use today, providing the different quarters of the three main towns, as well as villages and temple sites, with a continuous supply.

Architecture along the Rivers: The Ghats

Most settlements in the Kathmandu Valley are located on low mounds raised above the river plain. This provided the towns and villages with a certain degree of security from attacks and floods, and helped to secure the maximum amount of level agricultural land in the valley. The local inhabitants use the rivers for a range of activities, from washing to watering their fields. In order to stabilize the embankments and to provide access to the water at variable levels, many riverbanks along settlements and temple sites were firmly constructed in stone and furnished with steps, called ghats (figure 1). The ghat steps often integrate wider terraces and platforms at regular intervals. By providing a flat surface within the steps close to the water, the platforms fulfil a series of functions. They are used for bathing and washing, for drying clothes and produce, and for the performance of rituals. Many have been adorned with religious images and turned into open-air shrines. Certain platforms, in Nepal often circular in shape, are set aside for the cremation of the dead and the performance of funeral rites (*masa, tugah*). Ghat steps line long sections of the Bagmati and Vishnumati rivers and many of their tributaries, with the most elaborate bathing and cremation ghats at Pashupatinath.

Gateways to the Underworld: The Wells

Due to the elevated location of the Newar settlements, the rivers are not directly accessible to the people, and towns and villages are situated in places with very low groundwater levels. In order to counterbalance these inconveniences, an elaborate system of supplementary water structures was developed to guarantee a continuous supply to the inhabitants. Since the Licchavi period (c. 300–879), deep brick-lined circular tubewells were dug inside the

1 Ghat steps in front of the Mahadeva temple at the sacred site of Gokarneshvar on the Bagmati river.

Combining Water Provision with Beauty and Religion: The *Dharas*

In addition to rivers and wells, a whole series of interrelated water constructions were created to fulfil the diverse practical and religious needs of the local community. The most distinctive and widespread type of water structure in the Kathmandu Valley is a kind of *kunda*, a deep, stepped basin.[2] Early Licchavi inscriptions simply refer to them as *pranali*, meaning "funnel" or "water conduit". Today they are known as *dhara, dunge-dhara,* or *gaihri-dhara* in Nepali, and *hiti, ga-hiti,* or *lavam-hiti* in Newari.[3] The majority of *dharas* are made of red burnt brick, the standard local building material, with edgings, cornices, steps, and floors made of stone. Most *hitis* have a square perimeter, while some are oval, multilobed, or rectangular with an apsidal end. The basins contain a series of concentric terraces and usually have one stairway providing access to the floor of the pit. At the bottom, one or more spouts emerge from the lowermost retaining wall and provide a continuous stream of fresh drinking water (figure 3).

The spouts are either made of stone or gilded brass or copper, and are carved or cast in forms of mythical and symbolical creatures. Most are in the shape of the *makara*, the vehicle (*vahana*) of the river goddess Ganga, and then referred to as *hiti-manga*. By employing the design of the *makara*, the water of the fountains is equated with the waters of the holy river Ganga. The body of the *makara* is an open channel with removable cover, in which the water issues from the mouth underneath the recoiled elephantine snout. Frequently, the *makaras* hold in their open mouths a telescoping series of other animals, such as boars, cows, rams, tigers, or fish (figure 4). These signify fertility and the ever-reproducing potential of

settlements. They are known as *inara* in Nepali and as *tun* in Newari. Groundwater is the most reliable source of water provision and most town quarters, known as *tols*, have several wells located in public spaces. The draw wells have high stone copings and many of the top rings are decorated with friezes depicting lotus flowers, mythical water animals (*makaras*), snakes (*nagas*), and also representations of water-related gods, such as Vishnu-Narayana. Constructed on their sides are often small shrines (figure 2). The imagery applied to the parapet walls of the wells and the presence of the shrines, on the one hand, reflect the sacred connotations of the sites as well as concepts of abundance and fertility. On the other hand, they express the ambivalence people have always felt towards the destructive powers of water and the uncertainty associated with structures penetrating deep into the ground. Local myths and legends portray the well shafts as passages leading into the underworld and refer to subterranean spirits emerging from them. In this context, the associated imagery works as a propitiating force to counterbalance possible malevolent influences emerging from the wells.

2 A small shrine, expressing the sacred connotations of water, has been constructed next to a deep well in Patan.

nature. The neck-end of the spouts, closest to the retaining wall, usually depicts further mythical animals and divinities of the waters. Many of the spouts have artistically decorated tops, shaped in the form of lizards, snakes, fish, and frogs. Amphibious animals, real and imaginary, signify water and are believed to control it. Underneath the spout is usually a statue of King Bhagiratha, blowing his conchshell. According to legend, he is credited with guiding the river Ganga down from heaven to earth. Alternatively, there are representations of standing or squatting caryatids, often in pairs, who

5 *Dhara* in Patan with metal spout and sacred images enshrined in framed niches.

3 View into a brick-built, multi-terraced *dhara* in Bhaktapur, which contains a number of sacred objects.

4 A series of animals appear from the mouth of the *makara* spout in the Sun Dhara in Kathmandu.

appear to support the spouts on their upheld arms or backs.[4]

Placed in the retaining wall above the spout is the main sacred icon of the water source, drawn from Vaishnava, Shaiva, or one of the Buddhist sects. Due to the syncretic nature of many of the religious practices in the Kathmandu Valley, most *dhara*s contain a collection of deities from various religious groups (figure 5). Many stepped water conduits contain Buddhist votive stupas (chaityas) and statues of Vishnu as well as Shiva-lingas.

Drains in the bottom of the *hiti*s carry off the overflow, which is fed into large water-storage reservoirs and used to irrigate surrounding fields, or is disposed of by the cities' drainage system. In size and depth, the conduit basins vary greatly. The profundity of the structures is related to the level of the shallow aquifer which is being tapped, as well as its distance from the *dhara*. Where the water is near to the surface, fountains can be constructed almost at street level. More typically, a deep depression was dug, resulting in a wide opening at surface-level, and a correspondingly large number of levels in diminishing stages.

The oldest preserved *hiti* in the Kathmandu Valley, which has been dated by inscriptional evidence to 554 CE, is located in Harigaon. Despite its great antiquity, it is still functioning and in use today. Located at the northern end of Patan Durbar Square, Manga Hiti is the oldest existing fountain in Patan. It was founded in 590 CE, but what remains of it today is mainly a Malla-period (1200–1769) reconstruction. In fact, most *dharas* in the city areas were dug and embellished under the Malla kings. There is an important water conduit that belongs to the precinct of the Kumbheshvara temple (1392) in Konti in Patan. Its basin is furnished with sculptures from the Licchavi period, and is believed to be connected by a subterranean channel with the sacred lake of Gosainkund in the mountains of Langtang Himal.[5]

Water Features Connected with the *Dhara*s: *Tute-dhara*s and *Pokhari*s

*Dhara*s are intimately connected with two other kinds of water structures. Most have an overflow tank, called *tute-dhara* (Nepali) or *jahru* (Newari).[6] The stone cisterns hold about 10–20 litres of water and are either free-standing or built into the wall of a neighbouring building (figure 6). The reservoir fountains are furnished with spigots or taps and provide drinking water. This is only released when the water

7 Wooden pole with snake head at the centre of the waters of the royal bath in Bhaktapur.

6 Elaborately decorated drinking fountain (*tute-dhara*) in Tachapal Tole in Bhaktapur.

from inside the spout channel of the *dhara* overflows and fills the *jaladroni*-tank, or when they are filled manually. Many of the *tute-dhara*s are decorated with sculptural ornamentation in high relief or with paintings representing various aspects of the sacred waters. Particularly frequent are representations of *naga*s and *nagaraja*s (snake kings), the nine planetary divinities (*navagraha*), and auspicious filled water pots (*purna-kalasha*s).

Additionally, *hiti*s are interconnected with a network of *pokhari*s, large brick-built rectangular reservoirs, also known as *daha* (Nepali) or *pukhu* (Newari) (figure 8). Similar to the *tute-dhara*s, the *pokhari*s are fed by the overflow water from the *dhara*s, as well as by shallow aquifers and the rains. The *pokhari*s are the hydrological reserves of the cities, and play an important role in charging the urban groundwater. They have a permeable floor, percolating water into the shallow aquifers which feed the network of fountains and wells. Although the *pokhari*s were built as civic water supplies and are not primarily

8 The Rani Pokhari in Kathmandu, one of the largest reservoirs in the valley, has a bridge leading to a small temple.

religious, shrines, central pillars, and religious sculptures are commonly associated with them. Particularly noteworthy are the so-called "snake poles" or "serpent-timbers", in Nepali *naga-kastha*s, which are found in the centre of many reservoirs. They are wooden poles surmounted by a snake head, usually worked in gilded copper repousse (figure 7). *Naga*s are believed to be the regulators of the valley's water supply and the presence of the posts is intended to ensure a steady supply to the tanks.[7]

Civic and Religious Dimensions of Public Water Structures

Constructing ghats, wells, *dhara*s, fountains, and *pokhari*s for municipal use was a complex and expensive undertaking. As this was considered a pious and meritorious activity, however, many were bestowed by patrons to the public. A larger number were royal donations and the majority of them have *guthi* endowments.[8] At times, land was also bequeathed by a patron to generate enough funds to secure their maintenance. Every ward of the cities in the Kathmandu Valley has its distinct water features. At least once a year, on a day set especially aside for this purpose, they were cleaned by the community. This was particularly important with regard to the *pokhari*s, which can lose their recharging effect through the accumulation of impervious layers of clay.

Water structures play an important role in the lives of the people of the valley. In addition to providing water for their everyday domestic and personal needs, they serve as the social centres of the cities where people gather. Therefore, they were logical places for proclamations concerning the community, and a series of dated inscriptions is associated with them. Because *dhara*s are designed to accommodate large numbers of people, most have a series of spouts and an extensive platform at the bottom of the pit (figure 9).

Water-related constructions are visited for the observance of daily religious rituals and several have a particular religious or mythological significance.[9] Along with dance platforms (*dabu*), *mandapa*s, and temples, the water structures have been integrated into cities' open spaces and form stations on the routes of the *jatra*s, the urban festival processions.[10] Because *dhara*s are places of pilgrimage and ritual bath, attached public resting shelters (*pati*s, *satal*s) and shrines are often found in close vicinity. Through arcades, additional buildings, and sculptural representations, the areas surrounding water structures were transformed into artistically varied, rich architectural spaces, contributing to the structuring and embellishment of open communal areas in the settlements. Located on the periphery of the valley are a series of sacred sites, or *tirtha*s, found in the natural surroundings of the hills and dedicated to water divinities and ablutions (figure 10).[11]

Lavish Exuberance in the Royal Baths

Despite the civic and communal significance of water

9 A row of spouts provides pilgrims in the Bais Dhara at Balaju with freshwater.

10 Representation of Vishnu-Narayana sleeping on the cosmic snake in a tank at Budhanilkantha, Kathmandu Valley.

architecture in the Nepal Valley, there are also elaborate private water-related constructions. During the Malla period, particularly elaborate examples were created inside the palace precincts of the three royal cities. The basins served as private baths for the king and his family, and as sacred sites for water rituals.

A small but lavishly ornamented stone bath is Tusha Hiti in the city palace in Patan. The basin, commissioned by King Siddhi Narasingh Malla in 1646, is renowned for its fine sculptural decorations in stone. The small circular fountain is centrally located in Sundari Chok, one of the three courtyards of the royal durbar (figure 11). It is encircled by snake representations, has a model reproduction of a shrine facing the stairs of access, and contains a multitude of divine, largely tantric, representations. Presiding over the basin is a sculptural representation of Vishnu and his consort Lakshmi, seated on Garuda.

In the same year, King Pratap Malla of Kathmandu had a lavish basin constructed inside the Hanuman Dhoka Palace. His so-called "sunken bath", located in Mohan Chok, reflects in many ways the design of the royal basin at Patan and is also decorated with divine statues and a miniature temple.

Slightly later in date but remarkable for its shape and associated sculptures of snakes in particular, is the bath in the garden of the Bhaktapur palace. Constructed by Jitamitra Malla between 1678 and 1688, it is known as the Sun Dhara or as Thanthu Durbar Hiti.[12] The bath is rectangular in shape with an apsidal end, and has three diminishing levels of terraces. The basin is surrounded by a low *naga* balustrade and the curved wall in the east accommodates a number of framed niches with statues. A massive gilded cobra head guards this end of the structure, above the central gilded copper spout worked in metal repousse. The cobra is axially aligned with a wooden snake post, positioned in the middle of the water basin (see figure 7).

During the Rana period, too, water continued to play an important role in palace designs, as can be seen in the Singha Durbar in Kathmandu (figure 12).

Modernity and the Seamless Web of Tradition

Due to recent technological progress and the introduction of water provision through pipes, faucets, and pumps, a considerable number of traditional water structures in Nepal have fallen into disuse. It is noteworthy that although some are no longer used for basic water provision, and their utilitarian function has ceased, their religious significance as shrines and places of worship has on occasion increased. However, a large number of aesthetically pleasing and elaborate water structures

11 The intricately ornamented Tusha Hiti in the Sundari Chok of the Patan city palace.

are still in constant use. The fact that many structures, which were first established during the early centuries CE, still function, reflects the great skill of their builders.

However, modern technology is not the only factor that has led to the neglect of traditional water constructions in some places. A further reason for their disuse and disappearance is constituted by wide-ranging ecological change. Increased irrigation, the founding of new settlements which extract more water, and the rapid pumping of water in industrialized areas, have drastically lowered the groundwater table. In the Kathmandu Valley it has sunk by 8–10 metres within the past 15–20 years. As a consequence, many traditional wells and *dhara*s fail to reach the groundwater level and have either completely dried up, or only supply water during the rainy season. In some instances, electric pumps, powered by small generators, have been installed inside traditional water monuments to extract water from deeper levels. Although this extends the life of the structures temporarily, it will eventually lead to further lowering of the water-table. Near the slopes of hills, where aquifers are frequently located just a few metres below the surface, drinking water is easily polluted by rubbish dumps and industry.

In addition, drastic climatic changes linked to the warming of the earth's atmosphere which result in less reliable monsoon rains, have adversely affected the recharging of the shallow aquifers during the rainy season. At the same time, water basins which are badly serviced, or have poor drainage systems, have become flooded and the stagnant water gets easily infected with bacteria.

However, due to the problems connected with servicing complex pump mechanisms, often wholly dependent on expensive spare parts from abroad, a conscious return to the cleaning, repair, and eventual rehabilitation of traditional methods of water provision is noticed in the towns and villages of the valley since the late 1980s. Traditional water structures can be repaired and serviced at comparatively low cost by local people themselves. This understanding has also led to awareness amongst the inhabitants, of the value and beauty of the endangered heritage of water architecture in the Kathmandu Valley.

Conclusion

Water structures in the Kathmandu Valley are amongst the most beautiful and striking architectural features of the Himalayan kingdom of Nepal, but they are amongst the most overlooked and neglected antiquities of the region. Highly decorated spouts, religious statues, and miniature shrines have routinely been integrated into the walls of wells and basins, often combining sacred representations of Buddhists and Hindus, and transforming public water places into open-air sanctuaries. Due to the reliability of this complex system of traditional water provision, and the deep religious and ritual significances attached to the structures, many are still in use today. Ghats, wells, *dhara*s, fountains, and tanks continue to

12 Water channel in the garden in front of Jung Bahadur Rana's Singha Durbar in Kathmandu.

play an important role in the spatial layout of city squares and open communal spaces, the periodic celebration of festivals and religious rituals, and the practical and spiritual lives of the people of the valley.

Figure Acknowledgements
All photographs by the author.

Notes

1   The traditional names for these three cities are Kantipur, Lalitpur, and Bhadgaon.

2   The local *dhara*s represent a particular form of stepped basin which penetrates deep into the ground and in section resembles the shape of a funnel, in South Asia generally known as *kunda*. For further details on *kunda*s and their varied architectural forms, see Hegewald (2000; 2002: 121–47).

3   *Dunge-dhara* and *lavam-hiti* both mean "stone water conduit", whilst *gaihri-dhara* and *ga-hiti* mean "deep water conduit".

4   The sculptures of some of these atlantes bear dated Licchavi inscriptions and indicate the long tradition of such representations below water spouts.

5   According to religious belief, the basin of the sleeping Vishnu at Balaju is also supposed to be connected with the sacred waters of Gosainkund.

6   The traditional Sanskrit terms used to refer to these structures in inscriptions are *jaladroni* and *siladroni*.

7   At the beginning of the creation story of the Kathmandu Valley, the area is described as a large lake, inhabited by snakes. When, according to the legend, Manjushri drained the waters through the Chobar gorge, the *naga*s gained permission to retain their underworld palaces as long as they continued to provide the rains. For this reason, serpents are seen as the regulators of the valley's water supply.

8   *Guthi* endowments of land were made for religious purposes and administered by a board of trustees.

9   Ta Pokhari, Pya Pokhari (this has been derived from Prayag, the ancient name for Allahabad), and Kamal Pokhari (Lotus Pond) in Patan are revered as sacred sites or *tirtha*s, and rice balls (*pinda*) are placed in them when a member of a local Shakya or Bajracharya family has died.

10 For example, Pimbaha Pokhari and Purnachandi Pokhari are integrated into the routes of all the historical processions, the Gai Jatra, the Mataya Jatra, the Bhimsen and Krishna Jatras.

11 Prominent amongst these are sites such as Balaju, Godavari, Sheshnarayan, Dakshin Kali, Chobar, and Nau Dhara. Due to constraints of space these will not be discussed in this article. Many of them have highly evolved systems of multiple tanks and pools, containing religious sculptures and translating cosmic and mythological concepts and legends into stone.

12 Many *kunda*s in the Kathmandu Valley are called "Sun Dhara", which means "golden basin" or "basin with a golden spout".

Select Bibliography

Becker-Ritterspach, Raimund O.A. *Water Conduits in the Kathmandu Valley*. 2 vols. New Delhi: Munishram Manoharlal Publishers, 1995.

Hegewald, Julia A.B. "Water Architecture in the Kathmandu Valley: Function and Faith". In B. and R. Allchin (eds.), *South Asian Archaeology 1995*. Cambridge: Cambridge University Press, 1997, pp. 827–36.

— "The Lotus Pool: Buddhist Water Sanctuaries in the Kathmandu Valley". *South Asian Studies*. No. 13, 1997, pp. 145–59.

— "Diversity and Development in South Asian *Kunda* Architecture". In Maurizio Taddei and Giuseppe De Marco (eds.), *South Asian Archaeology 1997*. Rome: Istituto Italiano per l'Africa e l'Oriente, 2000, Vol. III, pp. 1455–69.

— *Water Architecture in South Asia: A Study of Types, Developments and Meanings*. Studies in Asian Art and Archaeology No. 24. Leiden: E.J. Brill, 2002.

Sestini, Valerio and Enzo Somigli. "L'architettura e l'acqua nella cultura Nepalese". *Antichita Vivà*. Vol. XXXII, Nos. 3–4, 1993, pp. 38–46.

Part II
VISUAL ARTS

Traditional Religious Painting in Modern Nepal

Seeing the Gods with New Eyes

Ian Alsop

The art of painting Buddhist and Hindu images in Nepal has continued for over a thousand years. During the last century, traditional artists developed several new schools, which have taken the painting of Buddhist and Hindu icons in new and interesting directions. This article will briefly examine the most important schools, and will touch on the work of some important artists of religious painting in Nepal in modern times.

Nepali painting can be divided into three formats: mural, manuscript, and scroll. Extant mural paintings in the Kathmandu Valley are now few in number and relatively late, generally post-17th century. However, there is inscriptional evidence from the Licchavi period (c. 300–879) which attests that mural painting might have been practised as early as the 5th century.[1] The most important extant evidence of pre-17th-century Nepali mural painting must be sought in the work of the itinerant Newar artists who were responsible for many of the greatest murals of Tibet and the northern Nepal/Tibetan regions, such as in the monasteries of Shalu, Gyantse, and Mustang.

The second type or format of Nepali painting is found in manuscript illumination: the Newar style of painting is first seen in the tiny illustrations of palm-leaf manuscripts from the 12th–13th centuries executed in a precise and delicate style, with finely defined lines and supple shading. This early Nepali style is largely based on Gupta traditions of the 5th–7th centuries, as is a parallel and related tradition, that of 12th–13th-century Pala regions of eastern India.

The third type or format of Nepali painting and the one almost exclusively used by modern traditional artists, is scroll painting (Newari: *paubha*), paintings on cloth which can be rolled up.[2] The early style of the manuscript illuminations developed further in the first *paubha*s of the early medieval period of the 13th and 14th centuries. These paintings on cloth are characterized by a formal composition of deities arrayed in rows, each with their own circumscribed space within the painting, filled with strong, bright colours, red being dominant. In the 15th through 17th centuries the style and execution becomes somewhat more informal, with the exactitude and careful lines of the earlier period becoming more spontaneous, if less sure. In the 18th and 19th centuries, Newar painters were increasingly influenced by the Tibetans to the north and Indians to the south. Hindu painting reflects more and more the styles developed by the Hindu (and Muslim) courts of north India, while Buddhist paintings adapt many of the conventions of Tibetan Buddhist art.

The *paubha*s of the 19th and early 20th centuries cannot be compared to the glorious works of the early medieval period. The drawing is primitive in comparison to the earlier works and there is far less attention to detail; the colours have little of the vibrancy and power seen before. This decline may perhaps be partially ascribed to the conquest of the Newar kingdoms of the Kathmandu Valley by an outside dynasty, the kings of Gorkha, who took over the valley in 1768. Although Newar society and culture continued much as before, there was a drop in royal and mercantile patronage as much of the wealth of the Kathmandu Valley was taken over by outsiders who were less committed to the religious arts.

In 1951 the Rana rule came to an end as a consequence of a civil unrest; but it was not until 1959 that Nepal had begun the process of opening its doors to visitors from the outside. Tourism eventually became one of the country's staple industries, and a significant factor in the resurgence of the ancient arts of Nepal. The coming of foreign visitors to Nepal has encouraged the foundation of galleries selling the work of modern religious artists, and sales to foreign residents and visitors often make up a substantial part of an artist's income.[3]

In the rest of this essay we will discuss how the artists of the Kathmandu Valley in the 20th century developed new ways of portraying traditional religious subjects. We'll concentrate on the work of a small group of seven artists who represent a much larger group of artists working in the various styles of the modern tradition.

* * *

The two most important religious painters in Nepal during the middle years of the 20th century were Manikman Chitrakar and Siddhimuni Shakya. Manikman Chitrakar (1903–87) of Bhimsensthan in Kathmandu was a giant of the early modern religious painting movement in Nepal. The Chitrakars, as the name (from Sanskrit "picture-maker") implies, are the hereditary caste of painters among the Newar caste hierarchy. Many Chitrakars prefer to use the Newari term for their name, "Pun", as favoured by one of the most distinguished of Manikman's descendants, his nephew Prem Man Pun (b. 1944), also a well-known artist.

Manikman was an extraordinarily prolific painter, whose paintings can still be found in the collections of individual families and various temples and organizations such as the *bhajan-shala*s, rooms where groups of devotees gather to sing devotional songs.

Manikman occasionally painted on canvas, but the majority of his paintings were executed on cardboard, depicting individual gods and goddesses, destined for family homes and altars. All were painted in his typical lively, quick, colourful, and relatively informal style. His *Vajra Yogini* and *Durga Mahishasuramardini* (figures 1 and 2) show an adaptation of the Tibetan formula of depicting the deity within a sacred enclosure, either a halo or a surround of flames called *prabhamandala*, against a simple landscape background. The background of the Vajrayogini shows a typically Tibetan symmetrical landscape, a calm sky punctuated by stylized clouds, while the background of the Durga scene has a distinctly Western watercolour style featuring a feathery cloudscape above a naturalist scene of hills and vegetation. The colours used in both paintings are powder colours imported from India perhaps in combination with some stone and natural pigments.

Manikman's most striking works were his narrative paintings often painted in sets, depicting various religious themes, usually Buddhist, such as *Jataka* tales or *Avadana*s which recount the previous births of the Buddha, or scenes from the life of the Buddha. A panel from one set depicting

the Buddha's life (figure 3) shows the young prince Siddhartha entering the family chapel while his father Suddhodhana and a crowd of courtiers and other subjects look on. As the inscription below, in Newari, recounts, when Siddhartha entered the chapel, all of the statues within came to life and rushed to offer their obeisance to the young future Buddha.

Manikman's fresh, colourful style is plainly on view in this painting. The technique is a variation of a gouache, although it is likely that Manikman used the traditional animal-skin glue as a binder. The composition is strongly influenced by Western academic art: specifically, perspective and a picture-wide sense of proportion are important elements, not previously seen in religious paintings. Most striking is the placing of the Buddha's life story in the context of then present-day Nepal. This set of paintings, of which six from a total of 12 are still together, were painted in 1940 during the reign of the last but one Rana Prime Minister, Juddha Shumsher, and it is the life of these rulers that is shown in the painting. In the background is a Rana palace where the members of this ruling family lived in Westernized splendour, and the uniform of Siddhartha's father Suddhodhana is that of a high-ranking Rana, including the Bird-of-Paradise feather surmounted crown. The Nepali onlookers are dressed in traditional garb.

1 *Vajra Yogini*, by Manikman Chitrakar, c. 1978, Nepal. Glue tempera, colours on card; 34 x 25 cm. Signed, *Chitra. Manikman Chitrakar Bhimsensthan*. Private collection. Photograph: James Hart.

सुंभ थी   दुर्गा ले औसासुर मारेको   असुं भ धी

2 *Durga Mahishasuramardini* (Durga Killing the Buffalo Demon), by Manikman Chitrakar, c. 1950, Nepal. Distemper colours on card; 36 x 46 cm. Private collection. Inscribed, left to right, *sumbha dhi, durgale mhausasura mareko, asumbha dhi,* [in corner yellow] *Chitra. Manikman Bhimsensthan*. Photograph: James Hart.

Manikman signed most of his paintings: this panel is an exception, but four of the set of six remaining bear his characteristic signature: "Manikman Chitrakar, Bhimsensthan". Given that Chitrakar is the traditional group of painters, it is not surprising that Manikman's family produced other important artists. His brother Prithviman was an artist as well, and Prithviman's son Prem Man Pun is an influential painter of the present generation, and the teacher of many successful younger artists. Several important Nepali painters of the late 19th and 20th centuries were of the same Chitrakar caste group, though unrelated directly to Manikman. The earliest is the legendary figure of Bhajuman Chitrakar (d. c. 1874), who travelled to England with the first Rana Prime Minister, Jung Bahadur. Other important names are Tej Bahadur Chitrakar (1898–1971), Amar Chitrakar (1920–2000), and Manohar Man

Pun (1914–95). Like Manikman, they painted in a realistic style, but on secular rather than religious themes.[4]

Siddhimuni Shakya (1932–2001) was a virtuoso artist whose works have long been considered the epitome of fine Nepali Buddhist icon painting. The Shakya clan of the Newars are held to be the descendants of the *sangha*s (congregations) of Buddhist monasteries of the valley, whose inhabitants eventually become lay householders, and in some cases trace themselves to the family of the Buddha himself. Nowadays the traditional occupations of the Shakyas are as fine metal sculptors and goldsmiths.

Siddhimuni was the son of Anandamuni Shakya (1903–44) who was himself a renowned artist and developed many of the techniques and stylistic devices that Siddhimuni later continued. Anandamuni travelled to Tibet, where he was

थ्वगुद्वोद्नमहाराज असंख्यलोकपि मुका देश्राजायाना कथ थेंदेवकुले दुह्राविज्याकल॥ ॥बोचिसतद्वाद्वाबिज्याना देवकुलयागु लुसासजवगु तृतिपलाताये माज्रनं देवकुले स्थापनायाना तयाथिं चैतन्य मदुपिदेवतायागुु जतिमा॥सुसुधा
लसा मद्देव नारायसा वक्सल्पे कुवेर कुमार वैश्वरा उल्लाउन आदिं लोकपालिपि थुपिसकले द्नाकथ्थे विज्याना वोदिविसत्वयागु चरणाकमले भोपुल॥ ॥थधिगु अद्भुत वरुखना शुद्वोद्नमहाराजा प्रमुवद्कदेव मनुख्यं
सकसारन हीली थधुध्यायागुु जुल धकला द्राद्व्यानान्वन॥ खुता उकारंभूमिकपमानमुल देवग्रायांथे सं पुथ्य ष्रिष्टियाना देवजाव्व स्थाना तुयीयुयामङललयाना देवकुले विज्याना ख्वंपिदेवता तिलंलोंद्रयात्॥ छ॥ ॥छ॥न१॥

3 Scene from the *Lalitavistara* (Life of Buddha), by Manikman Chitrakar, 1940, Nepal. Glue tempera, colours on card; 35.5 x 44.5 cm. The inscription recounts the incident of Siddhartha entering the family chapel. Private collection. Photograph: James Hart.

recognized by the 13th Dalai Lama as a great visionary artist. The history of the family records that Anandamuni entered a contest to paint an image of the 13th Dalai Lama, and, when he won the contest, was rewarded with a lifetime supply of mineral pigments which his son Siddhimuni inherited and continued to use throughout his career. When he returned to Nepal he carried on painting Buddhist icons, developing the unique style we associate with his name and his son's. One of his paintings entered the personal collection of King Tribhuvan, and is displayed in the National Museum, Kathmandu.

Anandamuni died before he could teach his young son his art. But Siddhimuni was inspired by his father's paintings and illustrious career, and using sketches and paintings that Anandamuni had left behind, he took up the profession and continued to develop the style that Anandamuni had pioneered.

Siddhimuni's *Vajra Yogini* (figure 4) shows many of the elements of the style developed by Anandamuni and Siddhimuni. The colours are bright, using the mineral pigments to their full and most brilliant effect. The composition adapts elements of the later Tibetan painting styles, particularly the use of a landscape background and a cloud-populated sky, but the density and opacity of the colours and the elaboration of detail are unique to this school. Particularly noticeable are the brilliant blue, green, and gold-highlighted rocks and the multicoloured clouds which show somewhat non-traditional purples, greys, and browns.

Perhaps most striking is the elaborate surround, a kind of *trompe l'oeil* treatment which suggests the brocade of the traditional Tibetan thangka.[5] In the modern tradition of Siddhimuni and his followers, the paintings were intended to be placed in a frame protected by glass; thus the elaborate brocade-like patterns were solely a decorative element adopted from the Tibetan tradition, without the functional aspect of a device for hanging and displaying the painting.

All of Siddhimuni's paintings feature a cartouche in the bottom centre of the painting, embedded in the faux-brocade patterns of the decorative surround, with the artist's name, and sometimes the subject of the painting, inscribed in a version of the decorative Ranjana script. Anandamuni began this practice, and thus the works of these artists are among the first Nepali religious paintings – along with those by Manikman – to be invariably signed.[6]

The majority of Siddhimuni's paintings are icons of single deities, and when depicting any of the peaceful bodhisatva figures, the drawing is sinuous and elaborate, and the figures are elegantly posed. In the *Vajra Yogini* (figure 4), Siddhimuni chose an unusual stance for the goddess, who is shown here almost as if crouching, when in most depictions she is shown lunging with her back leg almost straight.[7] Siddhimuni explained to Piero Morandi, who commissioned the picture, that he had already painted this *dakini* in the more standard position previously and wanted to experiment with this variation.

Siddhimuni died in 2001, and his son, Surendra Man Shakya (b. 1967), has continued the family tradition of

5 *Indrayani*, by Udayacharan Shrestha and Madan Kiju, 2006 (NS 1126), Nepal. Glue tempera, colours on cotton canvas; 71 x 58 cm. Robert Beer Collection. Photograph: Udayacharan Shrestha.

4 *Vajra Yogini*, by Siddhimuni Shakya (inscribed), c. 1980, Nepal. Glue tempera, mineral and dye colours on cotton canvas; 57 x 42 cm. Private collection. Photograph: James Hart.

painting. He is not alone in continuing the style of his grandfather and father; there are many important painters who have incorporated several or many of the elements of this seminal 20th-century Nepali religious painting style. The image of Indrayani, one of the eight mother goddesses, painted by Udayacharan Shrestha, whose visionary works we will examine below, and his student Madan Kiju (b. 1979) in 2006 is almost purely in the tradition of Siddhimuni (figure 5). The painting is surrounded by a faux brocade border in brilliant colours, (not visible in the photograph), and shares many characteristics with Siddhimuni's *Vajra Yogini*: a careful rendering of details, a naturalistic but brilliantly coloured background setting, and a realistic, modelled depiction of the form of the goddess. The landscape background shows a further development in several details such as the brightly coloured clouds contrasting with an unusual dark sky lightening to twilight hues at the horizon, and the naturalistic treatment of the tree, the stupa, and snow peaks shown in the distance.

Almost all of the modern religious painters of Nepal have been deeply influenced by the two schools represented by Manikman on the one hand and Anandamuni and Siddhimuni on the other. Many in fact acknowledge a debt to both in their artistic development. Deepak Joshi (b. 1963), the very successful

6 *Umamaheshvara* (based on the *Svasthani Mahavratakatha*), by Mukti Singh Thapa, c. 1995, Nepal. Glue tempera, mineral and dye colours on cotton canvas; 80 x 58 cm. Private collection. Photograph: James Hart.

modern religious painter now living in Swayambhu, at the age of 11, was "inspired and initiated into traditional art by Late Siddhimuni Shakya's classic Paubha Manjushree, exhibited at Birendra Art Gallery (NAFA)" and subsequently, from 1976 to 1981, underwent "rigorous training for five years under veteran Paubha Master Prem Man Chitrakar" (Manikman's nephew Prem Man Pun).

In the 1970s and '80s, two new schools arose to complement the influence from these two masters. I call them the "Newar Revival" school and the "Visionary" school.[8] The Newar Revival school represented the first attempt by 20th-century artists to revive the medieval Newar style of *paubha* painting that held sway from the 13th through the 17th centuries. This *paubha* style, which developed from the earlier manuscript painting style, emphasizes a formal and compartmentalized composition with only a few details drawn from nature; a lively palette using natural mineral and vegetable pigments, with red dominating; and finely drawn and executed figures often with complex textile designs in their garments.

Two of the veteran artists working in this style are Mukti Singh Thapa and Roshan Shakya. Mukti Singh Thapa (b. 1958) is a Magar from Bandipur, in eastern Nepal; in this respect he is unusual, as most of the painters who work in the Newar revival style are, not surprisingly, Newars. What is even more unusual is that Mukti is one of the originators of this revival, as he was among the very first painters to consciously draw his inspiration from earlier 14th–16th-century Newar paintings. A large painting, *Umamaheshvara*, shows Mukti's inventiveness (figure 6). The painting is based on the popular *Svasthani Mahavratakatha* of Nepal, a book recited by devout Shaivites during the winter months, recounting the story of Shiva and his first consort Satidevi and later Parvati. Mukti has depicted at the centre of the painting the Great Lord and his family – including Ganesha and Kumara – in their home on Mount Kailasa, the composition reflecting that of the lovely early stone sculptures of this theme found throughout the Kathmandu Valley. Around this central depiction are a series of narrative scenes recounting the history of Shiva and his first spouse, Satidevi, from the humorous tale of his stealing her hand by trickery to the tragedy of her self-immolation and his terrible revenge. The painting is not modelled on any previous work but was conceived by Mukti through the story recounted in this *vratakatha*, a popular puranic text in Nepal.

Recently Mukti has branched out, using the stylistic elements and traditional colours and patterns of medieval Newar painting to create new compositions that have no models in traditional *paubhas* but which remain religious in nature. His *Yogini #2* (figure 7) is a good example of this new development, showing a *yogini*, or *dakini* from an unusual perspective. She is seen from behind, and only from the knees up, in a dynamic, twisting pose. A large gold lingam (Shiva's creative aspect represented in a phallic form) is seen on the right, while on the left, issuing from a traditional foliate pattern, a swarm

7 *Yogini #2*, by Mukti Singh Thapa, 2007, Nepal. Glue tempera, mineral and dye colours on cotton canvas; 91 x 45.5 cm. Private collection. Photograph: James Hart.

of serpentine creatures rises and encircles the *dakini* before coalescing around the figures of a Buddha and his consort in union at top right. Mukti explains the imagery as related to the cycle of sexuality and creativity, with the feminine at the centre.

Individual creativity among all the schools of modern religious painting is burgeoning. One of Mukti Singh Thapa's students, Gyan Bhakta Lama, recently painted an unusual portrait of a young religious practitioner who lives, as he does, in the southern part of Nepal, and comes from the same ethnic community, the Tamang (figure 8). The young Buddhist practitioner, Ram Bahadur Bomjon – now 19 years old – is also known by his initiation name Palden Dorje. He has created a sensation and a large following in Nepal for his feats of uninterrupted meditation in the forests of the Nepal

8 *Palden Dorje*, by Gyan Bhakta Lama, 2006, Nepal. Glue tempera, mineral and dye colours on cotton canvas; 170 x 84 cm. Private collection. Photograph: James Hart.

9 (opposite) *Chakrasamvara*, by Roshan Shakya, 2006 (NS 1126), Nepal. Glue tempera, mineral and dye colours on cotton canvas; 68.5 x 54.5 cm. Private collection. Photograph: James Hart. Inscribed with the date 1103 (1983). 1st prize, 18th NAFA National Art Competition, 1983.

Terai. Gyan Bhakta Lama has shown the young practitioner under the tree he used for shelter for many months in the year 2006. The realistic portrait of the young ascetic and the trunk of the tree in which he was sheltered during his meditation transform into the stylized branches and leaves of the canopy, populated by monkeys and birds much in the style of Pahari-influenced paintings of 18th- and 19th-century Nepal. Above the tree we find the central shrine of the Buddhist Newars, Swayambhunath, with the five Buddhas arrayed above.

Roshan Shakya (b. 1960) is a skilled and dedicated painter of the Revival school, renowned for his painstakingly carefully rendered *paubha*s in vibrant mineral colours, of themes from the early medieval school of the 13th–14th centuries. His *Chakrasamvara* (figure 9) is based on paintings of this period from the Kathmandu Valley and shares the extraordinarily fine line of these early masterpieces. This painting depicts Chakrasamvara, the most popular of the tantric tutelary divinities among Newar Buddhists, in union with his consort Vajravarahi, against a background of flames in a central section which is surrounded by scenes of the eight burning grounds which are almost always found in depictions of this deity's mandala. Roshan's painting shows a reserved and exacting classicism which is equal to the finest production of the artists from the early medieval period that inspires his work. His use of mineral pigments is unmatched in the clarity and brilliance of the colours obtained, as is his mastery of the classical Newar line and shading. He is perhaps unique in the ranks of modern religious artists in his mastery not only of painting but also the various media of metal sculpture, including lost-wax casting and the considerably more difficult art of repousse.

Another younger master of the revival style is Purna Prasad Hyoju of Bhaktapur (b. 1962), whose *Preaching Buddha* (figure 10) is in fact based on the early, circa 12th–13th-century style of painting in south-central Tibet, a style which draws on many conventions from northern India Buddhist painting of the same period, but shows technical and stylistic elements that suggest that they may have been executed by Newar or Newar-trained artists. Purna's depiction of the Buddha displays his trademark execution of extremely fine detail, particularly noticeable in the fine gold tracery surrounding the head of the Buddha.

The other great school of modern Nepali religious painting is what I call the "Visionary" school. The masters of this type of painting are the brothers Udayacharan and Dineshcharan Shrestha. Udayacharan (b. 1964), the older brother, has created an extraordinary oeuvre of religious paintings unlike the works of any other Nepali painter. He works in close tandem with younger brother Dinesh (b. 1966) who often copies the original paintings of Udaya in such an extraordinarily fine hand that they are faithful and vibrant portrayals of the originals. Examples are *Vajra Yogini* (figure 11) and *Annapurna* (figure 12), both originally painted by Udaya and then copied by Dinesh; Dinesh's copies are seen here. We have already seen several depictions of the goddess Vajrayogini by Manikman

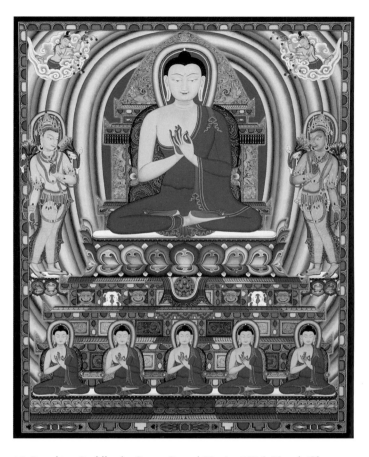

10 *Preaching Buddha*, by Purna Prasad Hyoju, 2006, Nepal. Glue tempera, mineral and dye colours on cotton canvas; 47 x 37 cm. Private collection. Photograph: James Hart.

(figure 1) and Siddhimuni (figure 4), and it is revealing to compare the varying treatments.

In both of these paintings, executed with oil paints on a relatively small scale, we see the extraordinary combination of realism and religious vision that is present in the brothers' work. Udayacharan explains that he does not use other paintings as models for his own, preferring to rely on the original written visualization, or *sadhana* of the god or goddess, to make his design. This of course was the original intent of the *sadhana*s, which describe, for instance, the appearance of the goddess Vajrayogini, who should be seen with:

> one face, two arms, and the red body which radiates red light brilliantly throughout the Dharmadhatu, the Ten Directions and Three Times. The right hand holds a hooked knife with a Vajra-stem. The left hand holds a skull cup fully filled with fresh blood. She is in dancing posture with a staff resting on her left shoulder…. She is like a passionate girl of age sixteen. Her breasts are full and large. Her three darting eyes are red and round.[9]

The flying stance in this painting is specifically part of the vision of the Akashyogini ("sky-*yogini*") of Vijyeshwari, whose temple is depicted in the background; and is the same stance shown in Manikman's icon. In the painting of Annapurna, the goddess's temple is also alluded to as the silver vase that is found in her popular temple in Asan in central Kathmandu. In these two paintings, Udayacharan and Dineshcharan have breathed life into these goddesses, whose youth, vibrancy, sensuality, and flesh are almost palpable in these works. In fact these artists have occasionally been criticized for the realism and sensuality of their depictions, but they believe that they are showing these goddesses as they were intended to be shown, as moving, living visions.

A detail of another work in an unfinished state by Udayacharan, *Gayatri* (figure 13), illustrates the almost hallucinatory realism of this extraordinary artist. The goddess's faces, each a different colour, almost appear to breathe; the eyes are alive and expressive, the lips full and gently smiling. The faces seem a vision or a dream.

* * *

Increasing demand from discerning Nepali and foreign collectors and religious-minded patrons now supports a thriving production of traditional art with an infusion of modern elements, but the future is not entirely clear. Many of the established artists bemoan the lack of interest in pursuing a career in the traditional arts among the younger generation.

12 *Annapurna*, by Dineshcharan Shrestha after an original by Udayacharan Shrestha, 2003, Nepal. Oil colours on cotton canvas; 91 x 61 cm. Private collection. Photograph: James Hart.

11 *Vajra Yogini*, by Dineshcharan Shrestha after an original by Udayacharan Shrestha, 1998, Nepal. Oil colours on cotton canvas; 76 x 61 cm. Private collection. Photograph: James Hart. The original by Udayacharan is in a private collection in Patan, Nepal.

Many students, they say, abandon hope of making a living in the arts in favour of seeking to go abroad to take menial jobs in the Middle East or in the West, or in a recent startling development, turn to dealing in land in the overheated Kathmandu Valley real-estate scene. But Nepal has already come close to the brink of the loss of its art traditions in the past, and in this author's estimation, the skill and talent on display today, in painting as well as sculpture, has not been equalled in the valley for centuries. May these arts continue to grow and prosper.

Notes

1. Pratapaditya Pal, *The Arts of Nepal, Part II (Painting)*, Leiden: E.J. Brill, 1978, p. 1.
2. Old Newari: *patibhahara, patibharada*. The modern term is a compression – typical in the development of Newari words – of the older terms which can be loosely translated as "respected – or sacred – cloths". The format of these paintings is analogous to the Tibetan thangka, and it is possible this *format* of rolled painting in Nepal developed from the Tibetan tradition, while in *style* the development flowed in the opposite direction.

13 *Gayatri* (detail), by Udayacharan Shrestha, 2008, Nepal. Oil colours on cotton canvas; detail approximately 10 x 12 cm. Private collection. Photograph: Ian Alsop.

3   Several foreign dealers and collectors have become important patrons of the new schools of religious painting. James Giambrone, who with this author founded Indigo Gallery in Kathmandu in the 1980s, continues to represent a number of important artists. Robert Beer of the UK, himself a skilled Tibetan thangka artist, and Siddhartha Shah, based in California, are enthusiastic collectors and dealers of the works of several Nepali painters. There are many important Nepali dealers and collectors in Kathmandu and Patan, and some of the most important collections of contemporary religious paintings are found in Nepal.

4   The dates often vary according to the source. We have taken the dates for the Chitrakar painters cited here from the October Gallery brochure for their exhibition *Radiant Transmission*, held in London, September 4–October 18, 2003 (online at www.coreofculture.org/radiant_txt.pdf). Another important source for modern Nepali painting is Narayan Bahadur Singh, *Samasamayika Nepali Citrakalako Itihasa* (Kathmandu: Royal Nepal Academy VS 2033/1976 CE). Singh varies in some cases from the information supplied by October Gallery, giving a birth date of 1907 for Manikman Chitrakar.

5   Earlier Newar paintings also used a cloth framework, but unlike the brocade-surrounded Tibetan thangkas, the Newar *paubha* was traditionally mounted between two simple pieces of indigo-dyed cotton placed above and below.

6   Earlier Newar paintings occasionally do bear the name of the artist, but as part of a long dedicatory inscription describing the religious circumstances surrounding the creation and consecration of the painting.

7   The goddess in this form is known in Sanskrit as Sarvabuddhadakini, and in Tibetan as Narokhachoma, the Tibetan name deriving from the Mahasiddha Naropa who first envisioned the goddess in this form.

8   These are just the names I have given them, and have hardly been accepted into general usage.

9   This *sadhana* is taken from: http://yogilin.net/efiles/mbk08.html.

Contemporary Nepali Art
Narratives of Modernity and Visuality

Dina Bangdel

The foundations of Nepali modernism are framed within the political developments of the 19th century. After the Anglo-Nepal War in 1814–16, Nepal established a strict policy of isolationism until 1950, for fear of external encroachment. Paralleling the British Raj in India (1858–1947), the era was one of the most contentious periods in Nepali history when the autocratic Rana clan singlehandedly controlled the nation in the manner of a medieval fiefdom. While they zealously protected Nepal's sovereignty from colonial rule, the Rana elites were fascinated with the West, consciously emulating European aesthetics in architecture, courtly life, and tastes. Two dramatic shifts in the arts mark this period. Despite its isolationism, the colonial aesthetics of England and France inspired courtly patronage of the arts. Further, a new genre of secular art catering to the Anglophile tastes of the Ranas prefigures the shift in production, from the religious arts to secular subjects. Specifically, the patriarch of the clan, Jung Bahadur Rana's (1817–77) visit to Europe in 1850 established Nepal's formal contact with Europe and its firsthand introduction to European aesthetics and arts.[1] Grand-scale courtly portraits and hunt scenes in the tradition of royal European portraiture quickly served as a well-calculated strategy to augment the Rana's aristocratic pedigree.

Precursors of Modernism

Bhaju Macha (Bhajuman) Chitrakar (d. c. 1874) was the first artist to visit Europe as part of Jung Bahadur's entourage. Bhaju Macha was trained as a traditional painter in the Newar style, following the legacy of his forefathers' painterly caste of Chitrakars. In his new designation as court painter, Bhaju Macha's assignment in Europe was to observe and gain knowledge of the aesthetics of Western portraiture, and to translate these styles of portraiture for the Rana courts. Bhaju Macha's exposure to European styles began a new idiom, with oil and watercolour as mediums, although it is difficult to determine the extent to which European art directly affected traditional Nepali styles. Bhaju Macha's most celebrated work, currently at the British Library, is a formal European-style oil portrait of Jung Bahadur, painted in 1849, and presented to the British East India Company. The Anglophile aesthetics of this portrait signified Jung Bahadur as the ruler of a truly independent nation – an ally, rather than a subordinate of the British. This preference for European realism also introduced chiaroscuro, perspective, shading, and naturalism.

The next generation of artists, such as Dirghaman Chitrakar (1876–1950) continued to follow their ancestral legacy as court artists and photographers for the Ranas. In 1929, Dirghaman was commissioned to paint oil portraits of the Rana and Thapa prime ministers for the Rana palaces, which included over-lifesize representations of Mathbar Singh Thapa, Bhimsen Thapa, Bal Narsingh, and Jung Bahadur Rana, completed in 1939 (figure 1). Atmospheric perspective, shading, modelling, and attention to surface design suggest Dirghaman's familiarity with European painterly techniques and standards.

1 *Portrait of Mathbar Singh Thapa* (left), *Portrait of Jung Bahadur Rana* (right), by Dirghaman Chitrakar, c. 19th century. Oil on canvas. National Museum, Kathmandu.

Chandraman Singh Maskey (1899–1984) and Tej Bahadur Chitrakar (1898–1971) ushered in the definitive beginnings of modernism in the mid-20th-century art scene. Their early careers reflected similar circumstances, in that they were closely allied with the Rana patronage, and as a token of Prime Minister Chandra Shumsher's benefaction, received formal art training during the 1920s and '30s at the Government School of Art in Calcutta. This opportunity to live and study outside Nepal during the isolationist Rana period profoundly influenced their vision and understanding of art. When they returned to Kathmandu, they continued to work under Rana patronage, depicting with renewed technical mastery the favoured elitist subjects of grand portraiture, hunting scenes, landscape, and still-life. Their modernist tendencies, however, are most evident in their introduction of a new genre of subject: the urban life of the Nepali community as a self-conscious articulation of their lived experiences as separate from those of the ruling elite. Modernity, in the context of Maskey and Chitrakar's new artforms, therefore gave agency and a voice

to the silent narratives of the common Nepali that were far removed from those of royal courts. As a signifier of Nepali nationalism, and more specifically Newar identity, this period of Maskey's work highlights the modernist concerns of national culture building. In *Tribute to My Forefather* (1966) Tej Bahadur Chitrakar masterfully renders a portrait that combines his classical style based on Western painterly techniques with a subject that reflects his heritage – the traditional profession of Chitrakars as *paubha* painters (figure 2).

Modernity and Nostalgia: The Art of Bangdel and Shreshtha

The 1960s marked the turning point for modernism in Nepal, with the arrival of Lain Singh Bangdel (1919–2002) from Europe in 1961 and his first exhibition in Nepal the following year. In contrast to Chitrakar's visual style, Bangdel's figurative and abstract works were radical departures from the established norms of Nepali aesthetics at that time (figure 3). Abstraction became his signature style, which he continued to

2 *Tribute to My Forefather*, by Tej Bahadur Chitrakar, 1966. Oil on canvas; 120 x 76 cm. Fukuoka Asian Art Museum, Japan, collection no. 1713.

3 *Untitled*, by Lain Singh Bangdel, 1969. Oil on canvas; 132 x 112 cm. Artist's collection.

experiment with throughout his life and which exemplified his avant-garde conception of a modernist style in Nepal.

His early figurative works in Paris, such as the *Muna Madan* series, however reflect his preoccupation: nostalgia for the past, and search for the homeland he imagines, but has never visited (figure 4). In Bangdel's articulation of modernity is a recurrent theme of nostalgia for the ancestral homeland and strong sense of Nepali nationalism.[2] This is not surprising since Bangdel grew up in Darjeeling, India, among the diaspora (*prabasi*) Nepali community. Bangdel joined Calcutta's Government School of Art in 1939, and stayed in Calcutta until he left for Paris in 1952. In the search for his individuality and identity as a Nepali separate from his fellow artists in Calcutta, he began writing his social realist novels, all portraying the struggles of the expatriate community in their attempt to survive in *muglan*, "the land of the Mughals". His search for his own identity as a "Nepali without Nepal", the nostalgia and longing for his ancestral nation, are themes that echo in his early paintings during the late 1940s and '50s. When he left for France to study at the Ecole des Beaux Arts in 1951, Bangdel's struggle was to find a unique mode of expression – a style through which he could be modern within a culturally derived visual language. In the 1950s, Indian artists such as S.H. Raza, Akbar Padamsee, F.N. Souza, and Paritosh Sen were also living/studying art in Paris, and each artist was involved in experimenting with his distinctive style. Bangdel was the first Nepali artist to study in Europe, and he strongly identified with his ethnic heritage. His goal was to produce something that would identify him as Nepali, with a stamp of his own individuality and cultural background, distinct from the Indian artists in Paris.

It was Bangdel's return to Nepal that enabled him to emerge as the leading abstractionist of his period. After his arrival there in the 1960s, with fresh opportunities to interact with other Nepali artists, Bangdel's international abstraction evolved. Among his later works, the *Struggle for Democracy* (1991) series is the most influential. Such narratives of cultural memory have similarly become important subjects for contemporary arts from 2001 to the present, with the depiction of images of the violence and political struggle during the years of the Maoist insurgency, culminating in the recent People's War.

Laxman Shreshtha (b. 1939) further realized Bangdel's experimentations with abstraction in the contemporary art scene. Living and working in Mumbai/Bombay for the last 40 years, Shreshtha has created a singular abstract style that distinguishes itself alongside the leading contemporary Indian artists, such as Raza, Ram Kumar, and Prabhakar Kolte. Born in the Siraha district of southern Nepal, Shreshtha went to Bombay's J.J. School of Art, then to the Ecole des Beaux Arts in Paris. He was greatly influenced by his teacher, V.S. Gaitonde, the forerunner of abstract expressionism in contemporary Indian art. Shreshtha's abstracts are characterized by large canvases in oil or acrylic, often as diptychs or

4 *Muna Madan*, by Lain Singh Bangdel, 1956. Oil on board; 96.5 x 78 cm. Artist's collection.

triptychs. Sweeping vistas and brilliant colours juxtaposed with warm browns and ochres pervade his abstracted landscapes, as if recalling the grandeur of the Himalaya (figure 5). Yet, undercurrents of nostalgia and memory subtly emerge as internal tensions within Shreshtha's juxtaposition of colours, textures, and geometric forms.

As with Bangdel, the physical beauty of his birthplace remains a recurrent theme of inspiration for Shreshtha's works. They are personal and spiritual, with a sense of nostalgia, articulated through form and colour. His early paintings from the 1970s and '80s often resonate with this sense of yearning and a restless search for self and belonging. Reflecting the fluidity of his transnational identity as Nepali expatriate, he talks about his career and life as a personal journey in search of the inner self, the notion of penance and sacrifice being present in his leaving the homeland that he much loved, his striving and his passion for painting, and finally finding success through creativity of expression and through interaction with his peers on the Indian art scene. Experimenting with media and techniques, Shreshtha's recent works more emphatically reflect his transnational identity. In contrast to the brilliant colours of the earlier abstracts, his recent exhibition, entitled *Elaborations* (exhibited at Mumbai's Pundole Art Gallery in 2007) included monochromatic paintings (figure 6).

Digital prints of the distinctive monochrome abstracts of the *Elaborations* series were exhibited the same year at Kathmandu's Siddhartha Art Gallery, after a hiatus of almost 40 years since his last exhibition in 1968. Indeed, it was a triumphant return of Nepal's native son.

Multiple Modernisms: From Mishra to Manandhar

For the next generation of artists, Nepali modernism was definitively taking shape through multiple contexts and diverse expressions, yet always within a culturally located framework rather than as direct derivations of Western ideologies. The works of four artists – Manuj Babu Mishra, Shashi Bikram Shah, Batsa Gopal Vaidya, and Kiran Manandhar – negotiate tradition and modernity in order to define their contemporary idiom in the global context.

Manuj Babu Mishra (b. 1936) continues in his 70s to be one of the most intriguing personas in the context of contemporary Nepali art. He creates works that are profoundly psychological, using the self-portrait as the dominant metaphor to explore the narratives of his inner psyche. His self-portraits are bizarre, the

5 *Untitled*, by Laxman Shreshtha, 1975. Oil on canvas; 127 x 127 cm. Courtesy Pundole Art Gallery, Mumbai.

6 *Untitled* (*Elaborations* series), by Laxman Shreshtha, 2006. Mixed media on paper; 66 x 101.5 cm. Courtesy Pundole Art Gallery, Mumbai.

face and form transformed and re-envisioned in his own idiom. His persona confronts the viewer as a demon, most often as Satan, Frankenstein, a satyr-like figure, or a horned Shiva, as symbols of destruction. In *Ramala with the Devil* (figure 7), the artist, as the horned devil, stares into the distance, while his wife Ramala, wearing her signature red sari, boldly confronts the viewer. Hindu mythic and Western iconic references are skilfully interwoven in the composition. Mishra's paintings often represent this type of visual play and subversion of the established Western canon, as in his *Mona Lisa* series. Here, the imagery of struggle, temptation, and destruction is accentuated by the subversion of Hindu mythic symbols: Ganesha, the remover of obstacles, either bears the missile, or stops it in mid-flight, while the ascetic at the far left is encircled by objects of violence. The artist's inner struggles are symbolized by the recurrent references to destruction, annihilation, and despair through weapons, missiles, rockets, and tridents – however, without the frenetic quality of form. Through such fantastic visual juxtapositions, Mishra's paintings are rich with subtle and overt symbolism.

Nepal's first avant-garde artist group, established in 1971, was known by the acronym SKIB, using the initials of the artists' first names: Shashi Shah (b. 1940), Krishna Manandhar (b. 1947), Indra Pradhan (1944–95), and Batsa Gopal

Vaidya (b. 1945). All four artists were trained in Bombay's J.J. School, and after their return, decided to showcase their work as a collective; they exhibited actively as a group until 1978. Each artist approached the contemporary idiom with his individualistic style; however, like Bangdel, their works collectively still embody a distinctive cultural character.

Shashi Bikram Shah represents a fantastic, symbolic, and surreal world, yet his forms almost always appear to pulsate and fly across the canvas with frenetic, raw energy. Shah's work often represents the notion of time, both eternal and historic, through the reuse of Hindu mythic symbols. For him, Vishnu's ten incarnations (Dashavatara) signify the cosmic cycle of creation and destruction, with Vishnu's role as upholder of order critical to the survival of humanity. His *Narasimha Avatar* (1993) powerfully translates the mythic moment through surreal forms, colour, and movement (figure 8). As the wrestler-like Hanuman looks on, the horrific form of the man-lion disembowels Hiranyakashipu against a red background while a rear arm gently protects the white form of Prahlad. Indeed, Shah identifies himself as a surrealist painter. His works are often characterized by his signature theme of horses. This again references Vishnu's future incarnation during the Kali Yuga as the white horse Kalki, or the passing of time represented by Surya's seven horses.

Batsa Gopal Vaidya (b. 1945) represents the neo-tantric artist in contemporary Nepali art. In the 1960s and '70s, Indian artists such as Biren De (b. 1926), S.H. Raza (b. 1922), and G.R. Santosh (1929–97) were establishing neo-tantric art as a means of expressing modernism in the contemporary context. For Vaidya, these tantric symbols were already a familiar part of his family legacy of working with traditional medicine and healing. His early paintings in the 1970s and '80s are vibrant and minimalist, with the focus on abstraction. In *Auspicious* (1972), a brilliant red square is situated against a stark black background, with symbols of auspiciousness, the *kalasha* (pot of plenty) and trefoil design, superimposed. Symbolic narrative is not emphasized; rather the formal abstracted qualities of the painting create the visual impact. As Vaidya's signature motif, Ganesha plays a predominant role, his abstracted elephant head being the subject of many paintings. In *Ganesha* (1989), Vaidya follows the same compositional format as in *Auspicious*, with a circle replacing the square; however, here it is Ganesha's abstracted form that takes centre-stage (figure 9). The tantric mandala is still present with the central red circles, as are the iconographic symbols of the eight-armed tantric Ganesha. Vaidya, with his bold, flat colours and minimalist forms, has transformed the religious imagery into contemporary visual language.

Another leading contemporary Nepali artist is Kiran Manandhar (b. 1957) whose style reveals a completely different

8 *Narasimha Avatar*, by Shashi Shah, 1993. Oil on canvas. Artist's collection.

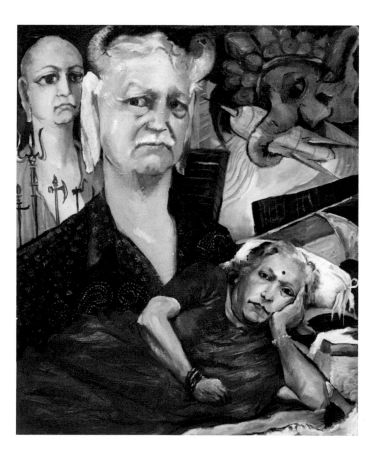

7 *Ramala with the Devil*, by Manuj Babu Mishra, 2005. Oil on canvas; 127 x 91 cm. Artist's collection.

9 *Ganesha*, by Batsa Gopal Vaidya, 1989. Oil on canvas; 61.2 x 61.1 cm. Fukuoka Asian Art Museum, Japan, collection no. 142.

10 *Five Elements*, by Kiran Manandhar, 1993. Oil, woodchip, thread, chaff on cardboard; 131 x 206.5 cm. Fukuoka Asian Art Museum, Japan, collection no. 661.

articulation of contemporary experience, moving towards a postmodern vision. Through his prolific creativity, Manandhar explores the definitions of international modernism through experimentation with mediums, styles, and subjects in order to create an expression entirely his own. With his art training in Bombay, Banaras, and France, Manandhar's works hint at his indebtedness to the established icons of modernism, specifically M.F. Husain, Picasso, de Kooning, and even Bangdel.[3] However, the execution and style ultimately reveal his signature idiom: daring colours, bold brushwork, and experimentation with mediums. His acrylic paintings reflect his wide range of styles, from pure abstractions that are intense explorations of form, colour, and movement to figurative works that are concealed within the abstracted forms. Beginning in the late 1980s, Manandhar experimented with surfaces other than the usual canvas or woodboard – Nepali *lokta* paper, glass, and cardboard. Increasingly, multimedia collages began to characterize his paintings, with the use of everyday objects such as wheat chaff, cloth, sand, rocks, and cloth prayer flags. His *Five Elements* (1993), along with his 1994 *Mandala* series, represents this exploration (figure 10). Five pieces of corrugated cardboard still in their recycled shapes are painted with colours symbolizing the five elements. Association of text and image are also present: blue/water; silver/space; red/fire; green/air. The exception here is that the iconographic requisite yellow for earth is substituted with brown, layered with wheat chaff. The dripping colours and broad brushwork rendered in swift energetic strokes both heighten the abstraction.

Feminine Voices and Postmodern Expression

As the profession of painting was traditionally a man's world, contemporary art produced by Nepali women speaks forcefully of a shift towards a perception of the world often centring around their gendered identities: of self, body politics, gender, and sexuality. The works of three pre-eminent women artists – Shashikala Tiwari, Ragini Upadhayay Grela, and Ashmina Ranjit – signify the individual and collective engagement in the discourse of feminine experiences.

Shashikala Tiwari (b. 1950), educated at M.S. University, Baroda, draws on themes of women and nature as her subjects. Her oil paintings reflect her technical mastery over the medium with her signature style of rhythmic lines and soft modulation of colour. Reminiscent of Georgia O'Keefe's representations of flowers, Shashikala has obsessively focused on flowers to hone her artistic creativity as well as her metaphor of femininity. In *Poinsettia* (1995), her subject is the single red flower, abstracted in its form, yet her treatment evokes a sense of poetic movement and sensuality in the undulating flow of colours. Tiwari transfers this lyrical style to her representations of women as she celebrates sensuality and femininity. Her late figurative work, *When Seasons Change* (1996) expresses a sense of freedom and self-confidence that is lacking in her earlier works, and femininity is celebrated through the dynamic movement of the female form (figure 11). Cultural signifiers of woman/goddess and her feminine sexuality are alluded to in the auspiciousness of the red sari and the joyous abandon of her dance, with the superimposition of the two faces accentuating the dynamic movement of her form. Here, the woman is no longer the object of desire of the male gaze; rather her abstracted form emerges from the background.

A world-class printmaker and painter, Ragini Upadhayay Grela (b. 1961) engages in the discourse on the feminine body as a space for the exploration of self. Yet, this search is located within the issues of social and political conditions. Upadhayay

11 *When Seasons Change*, by Shashikala Tiwari, 1996. Oil on canvas; 94 x 89 cm. Fukuoka Asian Art Museum, Japan, collection no. 1770.

Grela's experiences during her formative years in India, living with her progressive family who were in close contact with the exiled intellectuals and leaders of the Nepali nationalist movement, and her rigorous art education in Lucknow as well as Europe, have profoundly shaped her artistic career.

Upadhayay Grela's earlier works focus on exploration of her feminine self and challenging female stereotypes, through iconic symbols of Hindu visual culture. Forms of the goddesses – Durga, Sarasvati, Lakshmi, Kumari – are alluded to through the juxtaposition of associated symbols: snake, lotus, goose, peacock. In *Woman* (1999), the hybrid creature is fantastic but the visual impact of the work is heightened by the brilliant, flat colours and deliberate naivete of form (figure 12). Here, the divine symbols of the goddess are framed within the body of a bull, perhaps a visual allusion to the bounded existence of female identity in a traditional context. Sarasvati's goose *vahana* forms the horns of the bull, the male genitalia of the bull are transformed into Lakshmi's life-giving lotus; the *naga* hood emerges as a second tail; and finally the nude white body at the centre supports Kumari's peacock. The background, marked by the artist's own handprints, further alludes to a gendered cultural reference.

Her more recent works similarly provide commentary on the political situation. In her 2006 series, *People's Power: 1990–2006*, Upadhayay Grela develops the tropes of cultural memory to capture the violence, activism, and politics during the Maoist civil war, culminating in the April 2006 uprising in Nepal. Each work is deeply symbolic and iconographic, rooted within Nepal's political cultural identity, using familiar symbols and subverting their meaning. In these works, she conveys notions of time and place, however, through paradox and binaries: past and present; mythic and historic. In her *10-Headed Ruler* (2006), text and image create a complex narrative of war (figure 13). The form of the demonic Ravana, clearly alluding to the king, is created by newspaper text: "warning to the king; end absolute monarchy; violence escalates." Below him is the bloody clocktower, marking the date, "June 1", suggesting the inescapability of the event. By contrast, her 2008 series, *Love is in the Air* expresses a lighter side, that is at once a very personal articulation of her own experience and yet conveys to the viewer the essence of global culture. Again Upadhayay Grela juxtaposes a melange of visual archetypes of the East with images of popular consumerism and familiar cultural signifiers of modernity and tradition, of home and the world.

Ashmina Ranjit's (b. 1966) works question the definitions of postmodernity in contemporary Nepali art. Through paintings,

12 *Woman*, by Ragini Upadhayay Grela, 1999. Oil on canvas; 76 x 112 cm. Fukuoka Asian Art Museum, Japan, collection no. 1718.

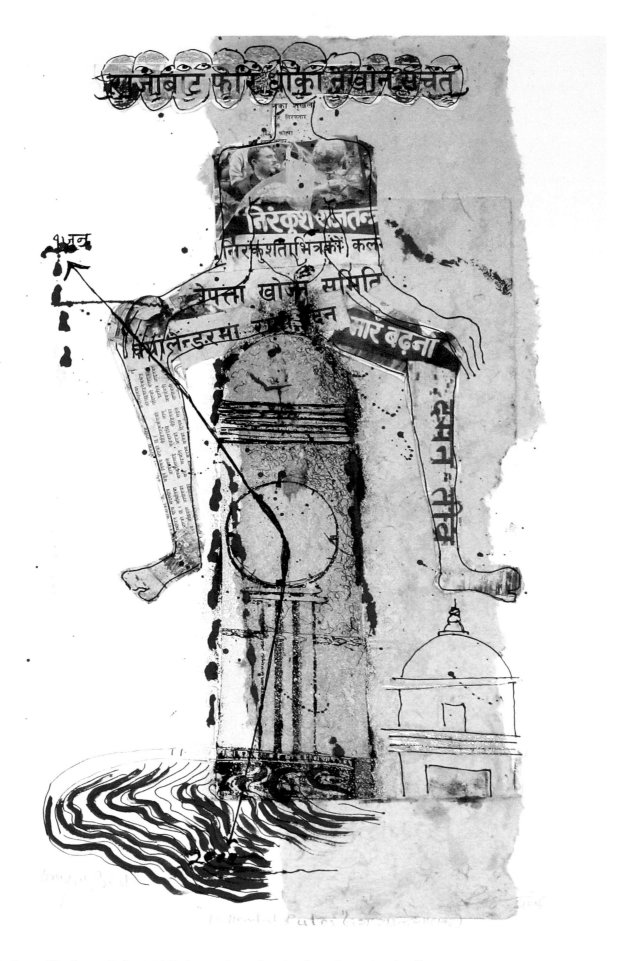

13 *10-Headed Ruler*, by Ragini Upadhayay Grela, 2006. Etching and mixed media; 49 x 34 cm. Artist's collection.

14 *Shakti Svarup (Feminine Force)*, by Ashmina Ranjit, 2002.
Installation, mixed media; variable dimensions. Fresco Gallery, Lalit
Kala Akademi, New Delhi.

multimedia and site-specific interactive installations, and
performances, Ranjit defines her art as a medium for social
change, in which she consistently interrogates, challenges,
and confronts cultural stereotypes. Hence, for her, the self-
referential expressions of gender, sexuality, and politics take on
global meaning. An avant-garde artist, she locates herself self-
consciously as a "Third World" artist, influenced to a certain
degree by the cultural "otherness" she experienced during her
art education in the West. Yet her subjects are located within
the cultural specificity of South Asia; hence subversion of
stereotypes, metaphors, and symbols are critical in her work.

Ranjit's *Hair Warp: Travel Through Strand of Universe*
(2000), *Cultural Body* (2002), *Shakti Svarup* (2002) series,
compellingly frame the female body as locus of gender discourse
– identity, patriarchy, and sexuality. Two specific markers of
Hindu auspiciousness and sexuality, hair and the colour red,
are used as metaphors to image the feminine experience. In
the *Hair Warp* multimedia installation, hair connotes the
multilayered cultural narrative: a thick, long, braided rope is
located at the centre of the installation space, signifying red
dhago (cloth hair braid) that defines a woman's identity through
her state of auspiciousness and sexuality. Sounds of the shaving
of hair signify the loss of status as widow. Similarly, in *Shakti
Svarup*, the red no longer refers to the auspicious *sindhur*
(vermilion powder in the parting of the hair) of the woman
as goddess or as wife (figure 14). Rather, red becomes the flow
of the menstrual blood that is at once unclean, dangerous, the
latent and forbidden symbol of women's sexuality, desire, and
procreative powers. Ranjit's subversive subject and presentation
are aimed towards a viewing experience that is not entirely
aesthetic but meant to evoke a distinct sense of unease as a
reaction to this represented body.

Her recent works deal with political activism and she
has projected the civil war in Nepal through site-specific
installations and public performances, such as *Adhikaar: Rights*
(2008), *Tamas: Darkness* (2006), and *Nepal's Present Situation*

(Happening/Installation; 2004, 2003). The latter, performed
in Kathmandu's Durbar Square and Ghantaghar, interrogates
politics and cultural memory.

***

At the threshold of a "new Nepal", politically and
historically, this narrative of Nepali modernity and visuality
must be contextualized within the parameters of these historic
changes of modernism. Similarly, the initial impetus of
installation art as a postmodernist metaphor in Nepal may be
attributed to the Nepali diaspora artist, Jyoti Duwadi, now
living in the United States. Duwadi's *Myth of the Nagas and
Kathmandu Valley Watershed* (1993) was the first installation
in Kathmandu that combined the valley's cosmology myth as
a context for ecological restoration. Indeed, for Duwadi (who
grew up in Darjeeling, Banaras, and Kathmandu) as well as
Mumbai-based Laxman Shreshtha, the most successful of the
Nepali diaspora, their art still reveals their cultural rootedness
in Nepali identity. As with Bangdel, whose arrival in Nepal
spearheaded the modernist movement, cultural identity and
nostalgia for the imagined homeland remain foundational to
the definitions of Nepali modernity.

Notes

1   John Whelpton, *Jang Bahadur in Europe* (Kathmandu: Sahayogi
    Press, 1983).
2   See Donald Messerschmidt and Dina Bangdel, *Against the
    Current: The Life of Lain S. Bangdel* (Bangkok: Orchid Press,
    2004).
3   *Kiran: Saga of a Modern Nepali Artist*, exhibition catalogue
    (Kathmandu: Everest Art Gallery, 2006).

Re-Imagining the Universe
Neo-Tantra in Nepal

Katherine Anne Harper

August 15, 2008, after a decade of bitter civil war, the Nepal Constituent Assembly elected the rebel Maoists' leader as the country's Prime Minister.[1] Landlocked between two modern giants, China and India, Nepal witnessed the decided demise of its feudal monarchy. Within the country's newly-configured political landscape, the population is multicultural, consisting of people from some 90-odd castes and ethnicities and speaking approximately 71 languages and dialects.[2] Slow to awaken to the industrial and technological age, Nepal began opening to the world in the 1960s and '70s and looked first to India and then to the West for modern ideas and technology. Television came to Kathmandu in 1985[3] and, since that time, foreign films, satellite television, and the Internet have released a flood of new influences. Instant global information and image retrieval has changed the character of society. Correspondingly, Nepali art has changed dramatically.

Traditional Nepali art was iconic, ritualistic, and determined by religious restrictions. Encroaching secularization, brought on by external influences and internal social change from the mid-20th century on, however, engendered new art for a new age. Nepali artists' roles and the art they produced have been revised in response to the changing world. In this essay, the work of 12 contemporary Nepali artists will be reviewed and contextualized. The works are grouped under the rubric of neo-tantra, a classification of South Asian art that depends less on style than it does on approach to certain themes and ideas. One consistent factor in neo-tantric art is the use of traditional Hindu and Buddhist ritual symbols of South Asia that have been recast in contemporary, transnational ways. It can be argued that, while certain aspects of neo-tantric art may be slightly indebted to the West, the work has an inherently South Asian spiritual basis that is its raison d'etre. The Western materials and format (framed canvases with acrylic or oil pigments) and the esoteric intent of the works (created largely for a public audience) have influenced contemporary neo-tantric artists. Nonetheless, the themes, iconography, and intent have their source in South Asian esoteric ritual art.

To understand neo-tantric art, it is important to address briefly tantrism. In the broadest sense tantra or tantrism is neither a religion nor Hindu-Buddhist mysticism, but a system of empirical-experiential techniques that are not exclusive to a group or sect.[4] Tantrism involves living rites that strive toward reaching enlightenment in one lifetime in order to avoid reincarnation. From earliest times, mystics and seers refined the supramental processes of meditation that allowed them to scrutinize, dissect, and classify the macrocosmic and subatomic universes. Their knowledge came not through the senses but through minute observations of patterns and sequences perceived through intuitive awareness. Meditation is a primary requirement in all tantric training.

Tantra's psycho-experimental techniques led to highly elaborate systems concerning atomic structure, macro-microcosmic correspondences, space-time relationships, astronomical observations, and cosmological theories that were given visual expression in abstract symbolic and diagrammatic images.[5] The esoteric tantric symbols were invested with ritual authority for use by initiated mystics. There are distinct approaches to use of abstraction between East and West. Tantric art utilizes coded religious and spiritual signs that promote fusion of the collective with the individual consciousness; in contrast, Western abstractionism is based on individual consciousness free from a collective sign system.[6] Abstract mantras and yantras, various mystical diagrams and iconic symbols, particularly those focused on the goddess and creation, are among the most vital forms of tantric art. While international critics often have voiced concerns that the use of abstraction by South Asian artists is derivative of Western abstraction, there can be no doubt that abstract tantric imagery was a generic part of South Asia's spiritual and artistic milieu for millennia.[7]

While the movement called neo-tantra may seem to imitate Western modernism, it is in fact linked to older abstractionism in South Asia. There is no exacting list of characteristics that are required for a work to be classified as neo-tantra; the category is largely determined by traditional subjects, symbols or themes, devoid of ritual intent, that have been reworked in a more contemporary manner and often utilizing non-traditional South Asian materials. It was in the early 1980s that L.P. Sihare, while preparing an exhibition for the government of West Germany,

coined the name neo-tantra.[8] The South Asian artists in the show were inspired by the world they inherited, each relating to tantric images in different ways.[9] That and later exhibitions of neo-tantric work met with mixed reviews. Westerners often look upon contemporary South Asian work with its rich colours, forms, and symbols as being awkward when blended with Western styles.[10] Artists in the West borrow extensively from other cultures yet are critical if the exchange goes the other way.[11] South Asian artists have been reviewed unfavourably when subjected to modernist art theory that regards itself as conveying universal scientific truth while judging non-Western art as the other.[12] Indian abstractionism, however, stems from an antiquity so remote that it cannot be dated with precision. In reconfiguring the ancient, esoteric tantric symbols, Nepal's neo-tantric artists are creating works that have esoteric spiritual impact. The artists provide glimpses of mystical truths that re-evaluate and juxtapose the material and immaterial, and in doing so become mystics who dream new pathways to the Absolute – in other words, they re-imagine the universe.

All of the 12 contemporary Nepali artists whose works are examined here utilize traditional tantric symbols and themes while employing a blend of elements drawing on transnational contemporary modes of expression. The artists by no means represent an exclusive group. What links them is their quest to convey penetrating truths while simultaneously moving beyond the traditional canons. Although employing some traditional elements, their works are far from nostalgic. The artists, nonetheless, recognize the great emotional and psychological power of things familiar; the pull of the familiar is the point where the artist begins.

One of Nepal's senior artists, Thakur Prasad Mainali was among the first to break with Nepal's rich sculpting tradition wherein the making of icons and ornaments followed strict religious canons. Having been taught to meditate at age 13, Mainali has sought personal and artistic inspiration through its lifelong practice. In his bronze sculpture *The Meditation* (figure 1), Mainali has simultaneously captured the process of the highest level of meditation *and* the bliss of enlightenment. The ovoid shape of the human head is represented at the moment of moksha, yogic exultation, when *amrita*, divine nectar, drips from the cranium into the open aperture or mouth below. The abstract form also re-enacts the macrocosmic process of creation itself wherein the male/female (Shiva/Shakti) flow in a perpetual process of becoming. The viewer glimpses the state of enlightenment as all merges with the unknowable infinite.

Not all neo-tantra artists so graphically convey exalted spiritual states. Manuj Babu Mishra's introspection results in phantasmagoric, polychrome, mystical visions. Mishra engages in an ongoing quest to understand the individual's place in the spiritual universe. His search is rooted in the notion of self. The artist isolates himself in his studio/ashram where daily he examines his face in a mirror searching for his soul. He paints his portrait in various fantastic settings that convey moments

1 *The Meditation*, by Thakur Prasad Mainali, 2004. Bronze; height 25.4 cm.

2 *Lingam and Stupa*, by Manuj Babu Mishra, 1998. Acrylic on canvas; 111.8 x 81.3 cm.

great looming mountains. Ganesha, an important tantric deity, visibly infuses the landscape with his omnipotence. Vaidya envisions the elephantine power of the deity as supporting the Himalaya and in fact the entire dazzling universe. Celestial palaces float amid a textured pink and gold sky. Ganesha's abstract features, depicted in vivid orange, dominate the crest of the peaks, his trunk spilling forward like a river of marmalade. The vibrant sense of colour, the landscape, and the folk treatment of the architecture present a delightful otherworldly vision. Vaidya's sense of self and nation, his cultural ethos, are yoked to the spiritual notion of the omnipotent divine.

Painter and printmaker Ragini Upadhayay Grela explores ancient tantric themes and ideas through a feminist lens. She affirms the feminine and the divine Shakti in her work. In 1989, Upadhayay Grela created a series on Kumari, the Living Goddess of Nepal, a theme that persists in her work to this day. The ubiquitous image of Kumari is seen everywhere in Nepal. Upadhayay Grela's powerful paintings drew attention to the discrepancy between the child goddess as the embodiment of pure power (*shakti*) and her extremely restricted existence. To Upadhayay Grela, Kumari is symbolic of both the repression of Nepali women and the creative feminine force itself. In her

of confusion and moments of subtle awareness. He asks, "Where is the God in self? Where is the Goddess in self?" He witnesses the animal qualities of the self (often the dog is the symbol of the inner beast) or he sees the spark of divinity in the self. He contends that we cannot know the interior without knowing the exterior of self and we are bound in the perpetual conundrum of visible/invisible. Mishra's painting *Lingam and Stupa* (figure 2) features a self-portrait presented amid classic religious symbols, indicating the quest for the divine. Mishra's fatigued countenance sports a bloody lip and is centrally located among other troubled faces that are borne aloft on the pericarp of a lotus. Above the artist's self-portrait rises a stupa decorated with the all-seeing eyes of the Buddha, against a golden lotus bud surrounded by a green lingam. The contrast between the serene eyes of the Buddha and the perplexed eyes of the artist hints at the human struggle to know perfection. The trail of blood on the artist's lip is a symbol of our material frailty. Mishra does not engage in traditional meditation, but he says of his constant wrestling for universal truth: "My brain churns and delirium takes over; the churning squeezes my brain like a lemon and the drops become my art."

A joyous mood is produced in the works of Batsa Gopal Vaidya. His brilliantly-coloured painting *Heritage* (figure 3) displays the elephant-headed god Ganesha merging with Nepal's

3 *Heritage*, by Batsa Gopal Vaidya, 2000. Acrylic on canvas, 86.4 x 63.5 cm.

4 *Kumari*, by Ragini Upadhayay Grela, 1989. Oil on canvas; 96.5 x 96.5 cm.

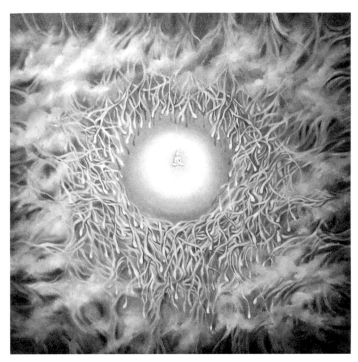

5 *Peace Mandala*, by Shankar Raj Suwal, 1989. Oil on canvas with oil pack press-mould relief; 76.2 x 76.2 cm.

painting (figure 4), the image of the child merges with peacock feathers. A saturated red, the colour of Kumari and *shakti*, is juxtaposed with the brilliant blue characteristic of the bird. The peacock, a sacred bird, is free to live, to dance, to spread its feathers, but the child is restricted by social convention. The longing eyes of the Kumari and the eye of the bird's feather merge; she has one white sclera and the other sclera is blue. Upadhayay Grela repeats the white/blue sclera for marking the third eye on the girl's forehead. The viewer is drawn to the enlarged eyes of the disempowered child. The *Kumari* series elicited criticism from traditionalists who denounced public exposure of the Kumari's contradictory position.

For more than a decade Shankar Raj Singh Suwal has practised the Buddhist *vipassana* meditation on a daily basis. He regards meditation as a way to instil deep peace in his life and to make meaningful journeys inward. There is no doubt that his work is informed and enriched by his practice. Suwal relates that glimpses of the infinite (*jnana*) occur to him during his meditation. His paintings are based on those mystical revelations in which he observes the flowing energies in the body as they merge with the universe. He creates luminous images of deities, both Hindu and Buddhist. In *Peace Mandala* (figure 5), the artist centrally locates the figure of the Buddha; made from press-moulded oil pack, the figure stands in shallow relief. Bursts of light emanate from the Buddha as he radiates numinous energy. Suwal is a master of fine oil technique. His visionary paintings, he claims, are meant to neutralize the negative forces of anger and violence.

The dynamic Kasthamandap Artists Group is producing some of Nepal's most innovative contemporary works. Founding member Asha Dangol created a series of paintings that were the direct result of his meditation practice. His painting *Tantric Dance* (figure 6) received Nepal's National Award. The work depicts a meditative dance related to specific tantric ritual. The figures were inspired by traditional Newari *paubha* (Tibetan thangka) paintings in which two dancing couples move to the rhythm or *tal*. Their attenuated hands and legs extend across the canvas in a moment of rhapsodic merging with the cosmos. The collage papers are from a traditional manuscript of songs and illustrations about the dancing god. Dangol affirms that his meditation harmonizes interaction between body and soul and that it is central in his process: "I did not know what I was doing; there was a direct flow outward, an unconscious flow with the canvas. Everything was flowing. The figures in the paintings have no hands or feet; their arms and legs extend in a natural outward flow to merge with everything." In his neo-tantric paintings, he began with the black background as a way to focus his mind and direct it to the centre. Black and red, the dominant colours in the series, are symbolic of tantric power.

Kasthamandap artist Sunila Bajracharya focuses on themes of women and their procreative capacities; she seeks to convey the mystical relationship of the feminine and the divine according to South Asian philosophical traditions. In her painting *Human Nature*, she utilizes the tantric *yab/yum* symbol of tantric sexual rites seeking spiritual fulfilment. Bajracharya's figures move beyond the sexual to hint at extraordinary ecstasy beyond normal experience. Her attenuated and abbreviated figures suggest the deconstruction of the universe so that a

6 *Tantric Dance*, by Asha Dangol, 2005. Acrylic on canvas with collage; 83.8 x 53.3 cm.

new reality is born. Her image is sensual in its use of brilliant colour, broad sweeping lines, and tactile surfaces marked with patterns similar to lines in etchings. While the subject is sexual, the abstraction and intensity of colours move the work beyond anything prurient or voyeuristic and the intensity of her vision creates a heightened sense of reality.

Erina Tamrakar of Kasthamandap also concentrates on themes of the divine feminine and creative energy or *shakti* in her paintings. Using women and natural plant forms as subjects, Tamrakar is able to create a vibrant visual connection with the mystery of life, the microcosm and the macrocosm. The inextricable connection of *shakti* and the miracle of becoming is explored brilliantly in *Woman in Nature* (figure 7). Against a vibrantly charged red and ochre background Tamrakar creates the shadowy profile of a woman in monochromatic tones. The powerful figure is the symbol of primordial creation. Plants sprout within her body, a symbolic device that can be traced to South Asia's Indus Culture and later to become one of the oldest of all tantric symbols. Tamrakar pairs plants and female forms in many of her paintings; in some, the plants unfold in zenana-like lattice patterns that obscure the sensual female form from public view. Tamrakar's females are the essence of Prakriti, nature's mysterious creative power. The artist taps

7 *Woman in Nature*, by Erina Tamrakar, 2006. Acrylic on canvas; 66 x 50.8 cm.

invisible forces and makes them briefly felt by the viewer.

The pensive Binod Pradhan, also a member of Kasthamandap, searches for the sacred in all things. In particular the artist utilizes the human face as the focus of his paintings. Again and again, he juxtaposes the faces of seekers lost in their internal meditative mindscapes; often he places them within sacred Buddhist and Hindu settings. In his *Inner Faces* (figure 8), radiant countenances merge in the constant flow and fluctuations of time/no-time. Meditating faces overlap and fuse only to form and re-form. The faces hint at states of transcendence and the glowing warm pigments suggest the heat of *tapas* (austere striving for spiritual enlightenment). The painting resulted from Pradhan's own meditation practice in which he experiences higher states of awareness that feed directly into his work. Unconscious feelings arise; they come from inside and are expressive of a spiritual experience that is ineffable. He admits that when he finishes a painting, he is surprised by his creativity. He says, "I do not know how I did this painting and I ask myself how did I put down these lines and colour on the canvas?"

Madan Chitrakar's work is a manifestation of a highly developed aesthetic sensibility combined with an imagination that is informed about the past, his culture, and his present-day existence. Chitrakar's recent works are his most philosophical in which he probes the very nature of cognizance and all knowledge. Thought is fast and fleeting; the brain swiftly and constantly adopts and adapts new information until it reaches the highest state of awareness. Referencing ancient teachings, the artist explores the theme of *prajna* or wisdom or knowledge (figure 9). He envisions a large hovering globe inscribed with syllables in Devanagari script. Like a giant air balloon, the globe tilts as if in motion, the result of being borne aloft by great gusts of wind. Fluttering red, yellow, and black banners, the colours of tantric worship, symbolize ancient wisdom. The sense of space, atmosphere, and movement – all allusions to the speed of thought – remind the viewer that, while we participate in time and space as does the written word, we may nonetheless aspire to the realm of higher knowledge outside the confines of our earthbound existence. Chitrakar is a descendant of an ancient line of artists whose primary responsibility was to create tantric art for royal ritual festivals. As a contemporary artist, he utilizes the inherited symbols in his works, but recasts them in a modern idiom.

The work of Manish Lal Shrestha is astonishing in its ambition and breadth of understanding. He explores themes involving the microcosmic/macrocosmic paradigm and the South Asian myth of origination. Clanging bells figure prominently in his paintings: according to Hindu philosophy, sound was the progenitor of all, giving birth to the universe. In his large triptych, *Sound of the Universe* (figure 10), several bells roam throughout the universe at the time of its inception. "Sound," Shrestha says, "is the heartbeat, the energy of all existence." As if viewing galaxies through the Hubble telescope,

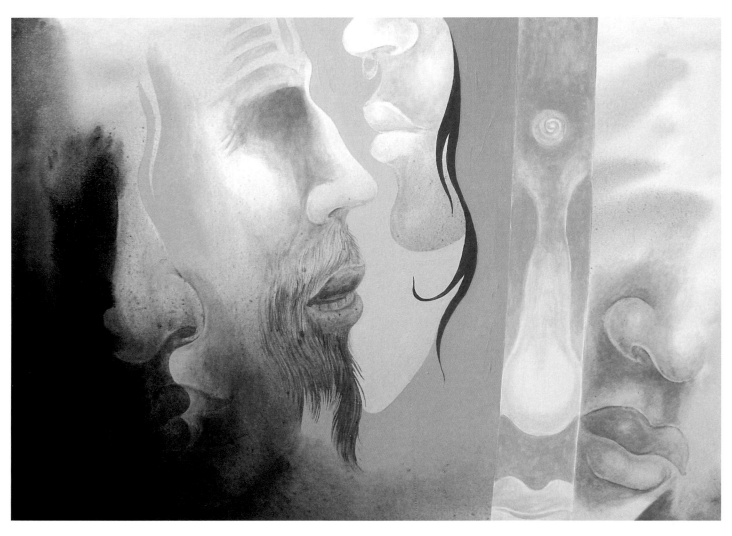

8 *Inner Faces*, by Binod Pradhan, 2006. Acrylic on canvas; 124 x 152 cm.

Shrestha paints great exploding nebulae, his personal symbols of freedom. Orbiting planets, moving circles, and flying circular bells are references to the never-ending process of birth and death. A mandala-like design of nine dots refers to the nine planets grouped in solidarity. A spiralling maze in a field of gold symbolizes the brain that has the facility both to measure logically and to attain full awakening. Shrestha does not meditate in the traditional manner; rather his creative process involves long periods of visualization in which an "energy builds up and then bursts out". He likens his creative process to a germinating seed. His stunning vision confronts the beholder with a glimpse of the infinite macrocosm.

Conceptual artist Jyoti Duwadi regards his art as his *sadhana* or meditation. For him "yogic discipline is the act of creating art and creativity is the quintessential spiritual pursuit." Many of his works are based on the abstract yantras and mandalas that are his birthright. He asks, "How can I not be influenced by tantric yoga, it is the tradition of Nepal." The artist notes that, on occasion, his works have been labelled too Western, something that he finds surprising given his cultural heritage. Duwadi begins a work without any preconceived

notion and lets it flow from his subconscious. He hopes that his art positively affects the perceptions of others by fostering inner realization. In recent years, Duwadi has created art installations that "capture the essence of time, as in tantra". In *Red Earth – Vanishing Ice*, an installation at the Sundaram Tagore Gallery, New York in 2008 (figure 11), Duwadi brings the viewer to a state of profound reflection on the destruction of the environment. He utilizes traditional Nepali metal ritual vessels, a block of ice, and a large painting on canvas (c. 4 x 5 metres) called *Shristi* (Creation) made from earth pigments, turmeric, and pine tar. Included in this installation are ingenious sculptures made from Nepali bamboo mats that suggest forms such as the *yoni*, the ultimate symbol of creation. Duwadi poignantly interprets the threat of global warming, the consequences of which are particularly dire for Nepal. Like a shaman, the artist creates a sacred, ritual space to focus viewer attention on the value of preserving the materiality of our existence by recognizing its immaterial sacredness.

There are two intertwining strands running through the neo-tantric works discussed here. The first involves critical misperceptions about the nature of abstraction in neo-tantra

9 *Prajna*, by Madan Chitrakar, 2007. Acrylic on canvas; 91.4 x 61 cm.

that need clarification. It is not appropriate to apply hegemonic modernist art theory to either South Asian or neo-tantric art because it is founded on religious ritual art that manifests an abstraction that is demonstrably ancient. In other words, abstraction *is* the iconography of tantric art and later neo-tantric art. The European-centred dualism of modernism is simply not applicable in that the non-figurative in South Asia precedes its appearance in the West by millennia. Art historian Oleg Grabar warns that today's historian should uncover the national or ethnic culturally discrete meanings of a certain kind of visual language instead of attempting to make them conform to an allegedly universal system that is a tool of cultural imperialism. He contends correctly that the history of art required by new countries in old worlds is not one that relates them to the West but "one that proclaims their differences".[13] Since the 1980s, the supremacy of modernism has been eclipsed somewhat by the more liberal postmodernist viewpoint in which debates about the authority of local vs. global knowledge involve attempts to move beyond Eurocentric ideas of aesthetics to emphasize otherness.[14] Today, as contemporary Nepali artists spread their work across the globe, they will not struggle to find authentic forms of expression, but rather for recognition from the rest of the world that they have authentic forms of expression that are eternal in their preoccupations.

The expression of eternal themes brings us to the second thread of the discussion: that the works, inspired by ancient

10 *Sound of the Universe*, by Manish Lal Shrestha, 2007. Acrylic on canvas; 182.9 x 304.8 cm.

11 *Red Earth – Vanishing Ice*, by Jyoti Duwadi. Installation at the Sundaram Tagore Gallery, New York, April–May 2008. Mixed media; variable dimensions.

spiritual traditions, have an authority that should not be quickly dismissed. In facing the emptiness of globalization, environmental disaster, and accelerating secularization, neo-tantric artists have created silent reminders of the Absolute. In doing so, they have made information available that is not readily accessible from other sources and that brings the viewer to a level of reality that is otherwise unreachable.[15] Each artist fulfils a role as artist-shaman by linking artistry and religiosity.[16] Their works, although created for a secular audience and without obvious religious content, re-imagine and reify the spiritual universe and the human place within its cycles. Such sophisticated hybrids emphasize the pure essence of existence as well as affirm the internationalism of Nepali artists. Their works affirm all that is positive, enduring, and unique about Nepal and, in fact, such arresting work could be regarded as modern *upaya* or expedient means for discerning the Absolute. In other words, the works provoke moments of existential clarity.

One definition of existentialism is the human attempt to describe existence, its conflicts, and the anticipation of superseding them.[17] Neo-tantric work may lead the viewer to an existential moment when time is arrested and there is a profound knowing of something greater than self. It is an awareness that glimpses at answers to the unknowns of the cyclic universe and the human predicament subject to transitoriness, but with a clear recognition of its corollary that simultaneous with perishing is becoming.[18] What is distinctive about the neo-tantric work is its profound humanism, and its lack of self-consciousness, cynicism, anger, and angst. The works provide the viewer with an opportunity to reclaim lost wisdom.

Acknowledgements

For her help and many insights, I extend my gratitude to Sangeeta Thapa, art historian, patron, and inspiration to artists and to all who appreciate contemporary Nepali art. In addition, I remember also with heartfelt thanks the many artists I interviewed for this article who so generously shared their work and ideas.

Notes

1   Tilak Pokharel and Somini Sengupta, "Nepal Elects a Maoist to Be the Prime Minister", *New York Times* (August 16, 2008, National Edition).

2   Manjushri Thapa, *Forget Kathmandu: An Elegy for Democracy* (New Delhi: Penguin Books, 2007), p. 2.

3   Ibid., p. 115.

4   Ajit Mookerjee and Madhu Khanna, *The Tantric Way: Art, Science, Ritual* (Boston: New York Graphic Society, 1977), p. 14.

5   Ibid.

6   Virginia Whiles, "Tantric Imagery: Affinities with Twentieth Century Abstract Art", *Studio International*, 181 (March 1971), p. 100.

7   Thomas McEvilley, *Art and Otherness: Crisis in Cultural Identity* (Kingston, New York: McPherson & Company, 1992), pp. 117–18.

8   L.P. Sihare, *Tantra: Philosophie und Bildidee, Spekte zeitgonossischer indischer Kunst* (Stuttgart: Institut fur Auslandsbeziehunger, 1983), p. 1.

9   Edith A. Tonelli, *Neo-Tantra: Contemporary Indian Painting Inspired by Tradition* (Los Angeles: University of California, 1985), p. 11.

10 Vishakha N. Desai, "Reorienting Ourselves to Asian Art", *Art News* (November 1996), p. 152.

11 Holland Cotter, "The Brave New Face of Art from the East", *New York Times* (September 29, 1996, The Arts).

12 McEvilley, p. 11.

13 Oleg Grabar, "On the Universality of the History of Art", *Art Journal*, 42/4 (Winter 1982), p. 281.

14 McEvilley, p. 86.

15 Paul Tillich, "Existential Aspects of Modern Art", in Carl Michalson (ed.), *Christianity and the Existentialists* (New York: Charles Scribner's Sons, 1956), p. 146.

16 Donald Preziosi, "Enchanted Credulities: Art, Religion, and Amnesia", *X-Tra*, 11/1 (Fall 2008), p. 24.

17 Tillich, p. 129.

18 Hans-Georg Gadamer, "The Continuity of History and the Existential Moment", *Philosophy Today*, 16/3 (Fall 1972), p. 233.

The Potters of Thimi
Village Ceramic Traditions in Flux

Ani Kasten

The village of Thimi, located between Kathmandu and Bhaktapur on the Arniko Highway, is a traditional centre for pottery-making in the Kathmandu Valley. Thimi is one of the oldest and most important pottery-making villages of Nepal. Located approximately 11 kilometres from Kathmandu, it is still home to around 10,000 of Nepal's potters, who have been working there for centuries, following their traditional caste occupation. Today the village is composed of nearly 2,000 potters' workshops run by families who are members of the Newar Kumale caste, bearing the surname Prajapati. The potters are subsistence farmers, alternating seasonally between agricultural work and supplying Nepali households with goods made from clay on the potter's wheel. The proximity of the potters' workshops to one another, as well as the shared caste traditions of the families, has created a working environment of cooperation that has existed for hundreds of years in the village. Within this environment, the development of the pottery tradition has been a community concern rather than a struggle for individual success.

Little innovation has taken place in the methods of pottery-making, aside from a few NGO-led projects to introduce new technology into some of the workshops. Yet, many challenges have arisen for the potters' way of life in Thimi. There has been a considerable drop in demand for pottery goods due to the wide availability of metal and plastic kitchen utensils that has eroded much of the market for clay pots. Also, on account of the changing needs of society around them, many of the younger generation in Thimi have questioned the sustainability of the potters' craft as a mainstay of the village economy, and have begun to drift away from the family occupation as it has existed for hundreds of years. Many of the older generation feel a distinct sense of loss as their traditional way of life is threatened with extinction.

In response to the desire to preserve this unique way of life (a desire shared by the inhabitants of Thimi, other Nepali groups, and some foreign development organizations), several projects are underway in the village to help make the ceramics produced there more relevant to the needs of a contemporary market economy. Examining the history of ceramic development in the village over the past 30 years illuminates the ways in which the potters' culture can and must be preserved in Thimi through modernization, as well as the ways in which modernization necessarily changes this traditional culture, incurring a certain degree of loss.

Wandering through the streets of Purano Thimi (Old Thimi), one is struck by the extent to which the village has been preserved as a pottery-producing centre since ancient times. The tiny alleys paved with brick meander through courtyards filled with villagers conducting all manner of pottery processes, from forming the pots with a wooden paddle, to drying them and firing them in traditional straw kilns (figure 1). One also sees people threshing rice by hand, washing clothes in big clay tubs and drying them in the sun, cleaning and bundling vegetables to get them ready to take to market, and sitting inside of the darkened doorways of their homes made from wooden beams, brick, and mud, smoking from a water pipe and gossiping with the neighbours. It is as if time stopped five centuries ago. The occasional rasping engine of a motorbike or tractor, or a tiny sign advertising international phone calls and an Internet connection are the only reminders that the village has entered the 21st century.

In every courtyard and flanking the narrow alleys are stacks of red and black clay pots in various shapes and sizes awaiting transport to market (figure 2), and large straw bales for use in building the kilns (figure 3), with ducks wallowing in the murky puddles and dogs napping with their pups nearby. The traditional potterywares of Thimi are all produced from the red earthenware clay indigenous to the Kathmandu Valley. Potters venture out to farmers' paddies several times a year and dig clay from beneath the topsoil layer. Most of the workshops in Thimi are contained in mud-walled rooms with no electricity or running water. Potters do everything by hand, beginning with mixing their clay, which they hack into small pieces, moisten with water to the proper consistency, and then mix by stomping on it vigorously with their feet. Then the clay is kneaded with the hands to remove as much air as possible before forming it

into pots on huge wheels made of concrete-filled truck tyres set into the ground on a ball-bearing (figure 4). The wheels were traditionally made from wooden planks joined and cut into a large circle, approximately 1.5 metres in diameter, but as wood became more costly and scarce, the truck tyre filled with concrete was one of the potters' innovations.

The potter stands over the wheel and sets it turning on the bearing with a long pole (figure 5). Once maximum speed is achieved, he puts the stick aside and the momentum of the heavy concrete allows him to throw one or two very crude pots before he must set the wheel turning again. Pots are dried in the sun (figure 6) and then smoke-fired within a large stack of straw and pot shards covered in ash (figure 7). The traditional unglazed pottery of Nepal consists mostly of flowerpots (figure 8), pitchers and jars for storage of water and grain (figures 9 and 10), large vessels for distilling rice spirits called *rakshi*, and cooking pots, although these have been eclipsed for the most part by metal ones. These are the wares that have been produced in Thimi for centuries, and thousands of potters there still work in this way. They manage to survive on the little they

1 A straw kiln being unloaded in a courtyard in Thimi, while just-formed flowerpots dry in the sun.

2 Finished wares stacked outside a home in Thimi.

neighbours often fire their pots together in a single, large kiln, and everyone participates in the unloading, once the pots are cool. It is the men who transport the pots to market, and barter or sell them.

As more Nepalis prefer to buy metal and plastic goods, it has become increasingly difficult for the potters to earn a living in the traditional way. Thus, much of the younger generation has opted instead for tailoring careers, or found work driving taxis in the city. Because of caste oppression, and a general lack of appreciation for the pottery-making tradition in Thimi, young villagers are quick to leave their family occupation for jobs in finance, business, or Internet technology if they are fortunate enough to afford an education in those subjects. Because of this attitude, as well as the general economic malaise in the village, development of the pottery-making profession has been rather slow, and many of the older villagers in Thimi have become increasingly concerned that their ancient craft tradition will become extinct as more young people depart in search of better economic opportunities. This concern has fostered in some families the desire to modernize, and many of the inhabitants of Thimi have come to believe that their ancient culture cannot survive without change. Thus some modern technological advances have begun to take hold in the village and have offered the hope of preserving this unique craft tradition in its place of origin.

Thimi Potters' Cooperative and the CPPN

The pottery industry in Nepal has been one of the most underdeveloped in the world, lagging far behind its neighbours China and India in terms of methods and technology. In 1982, 40 of the pottery workshops in Thimi banded together with the help of the Nepal government in cooperation with a German

can make, loading the pots onto a wooden yoke worn across the shoulders, and carrying them on foot from village to village during harvest time, where they trade pots for a year's supply of rice. Wealthier potters who have a larger production capacity will sometimes hire a truck and load hundreds of pots into the back, taking them as far away as Gorkha.[1]

The daily tasks in the potteries of Thimi are performed by all members of the family, both men and women, and often children when they have time off from school, and are sometimes divided up according to gender. Women never work at the wheel, nor do they form the pots with the traditional paddling technique that potters use for the larger forms. The large paddled pots are built from thick, flat coils, pressed one on top of each other as they become dry enough to support the weight of another coil layer. Once the rudimentary form is made, the potter then walks in a circle around the pot, and paddles the sides with a wooden mallet. The inner form is supported by a rounded anvil held in his other hand. In this way, the walls are made thinner and the shape refined. These practices in forming pots are always performed by men. Women are then enlisted for the finishing techniques, such as refining the bottoms of the pots as they are removed from the wheel, painting on a dark red decoration made from terra sigilatta,[2] and stamping decorations around the rims of the pots with handmade wooden stamps dipped in white talc. Men and women build and load the traditional straw kilns together, and tend to the firing, which lasts for four days. Groups of

3 Bales of straw stacked on either side of a road in Thimi.

4 A young potter throwing a flower pot on a truck-tyre pottery wheel. Photograph © Dinodia.

5 Potter turning an old-style Nepali pottery wheel with a wooden pole. Photograph © Dinodia.

aid organization called GTZ Project, and founded the Ceramics Promotion Project of Nepal (CPPN). Through the CPPN, the Thimi Bhaktapur Potters' Cooperative was formed in an effort to begin modernizing the pottery industry. For nine years after that, the CPPN appointed an American potter by the name of Jim Danisch to work with the local cooperative on introducing the electric wheel, developing modern oil-fired kilns made from local bricks and mortar mixed with rice husks,[3] and creating low-fire, leadless glazes to suit the indigenous earthenware clay body. Nepali potters began using glaze for the first time in 1987. To give some idea of the lag in ceramic development in Nepal, one must consider that archaeologists have excavated glazed pot shards in China from sites dating back to 1500 BCE.

The CPPN is notable for its dedication to keeping the technological advances locally sustainable, and it began by introducing a locally manufactured wheel that runs on a simple motor attached to a foot pedal that, when pressed intermittently, turns a large concrete flywheel. When the CPPN first conducted a demonstration of the new machine in the town square in Thimi, many of the older potters were sceptical and refused to try the wheel. However, it was adopted by several of the newer workshops, and has slowly caught on in much of the village. There are still many workshops in Thimi

that prefer to use the traditional wheel and have not made any upgrades to their technology. This is dually because of lack of funds and nostalgia for the old way of life. The Thimi potters who have been making pottery in the old way may have felt their tradition challenged when suddenly faced with change. Making the transition from an age-old tradition with which they are familiar and getting comfortable with a new technology, however small or simple, require some learning and behavioural adjustments which the potters might have found difficult.

The CPPN also began building brick kilns that are fired with a locally produced burner designed specially for the project. The kiln consists of a large chamber with shelves on which the wares are loaded, and a smaller fire-box chamber beneath where the burners send heat into the kiln that is then circulated evenly throughout the firing chamber. The burner runs on a kerosene drip that is ignited through contact with pressurized steam, sending a flame into the kiln capable of reaching temperatures of above 1240°C. With this new kiln model, potters were able to produce colourful glazed ware for the home and garden. The traditional straw kiln is only able to reach a temperature of approximately 700°C, and it is not possible to fire glazed ware at such a low temperature.

In 1987, the Thimi Potters' Cooperative began to create low-fire, glazed ware made from local and Indian materials for sale to tourist hotels and restaurants in Nepal, as well as to shops carrying handicrafts made in Nepal. The range of goods produced by member workshops include all manner of plates, cups, bowls, teapots, serving dishes, as well as incense-holders, candlesticks, lamp-bases, vases, and colourfully decorated garden pots. The market for these products consists primarily of expatriates living in Kathmandu, tourists, upmarket hotels and restaurants, as well as a small export market. The modernization of these workshops in Thimi raised the quality of goods produced there, and prices increased as well. Many Nepali households were not willing to pay such high prices for ceramic goods. The mindset of Nepali culture with regard to clay wares produced in Thimi has been that ceramic is a low-quality material used for producing disposable, utilitarian objects for the kitchen. Nepalis have been slow to adapt to the idea of quality, high-end wares made of ceramic that offer beauty as well as utility in the home.

Within nine years, the CPPN succeeded in its goal of helping to develop a self-sufficient potters' cooperative as well as planting the seeds for a local market for wares produced by the member workshops. Once all loans for materials and equipment

6 Flowerpots and jars drying in the sun. Photograph © Dinodia.

granted by the project were paid off in revenues coming into the cooperative, the CPPN ended in 1991.

Thimi Ceramics

While much of Thimi still remains distinctly traditional, about seven of the workshops in the Cooperative have continued using modern methods in earnest. Thimi Ceramics is one of these seven pioneering workshops. It was founded by Santa Bahadur Prajapati and his two sons, Santa Kumar and Laxmi Kumar. While participating in the CPPN, the two young brothers pursued training abroad in India and Thailand, and then, with the help of the CPPN, established their own pottery in 1985. Having gathered experience from their training in other countries, the two brothers had developed many new ideas for a more modern approach to ceramics. Thimi Ceramics was one of the first workshops to incorporate the new electric wheels and oil-fired brick kilns, and began making the first glazed earthenware in 1987.

Santa and Laxmi Kumar have always believed strongly in preserving the tradition of pottery made by hand. In their minds, and in the minds of many who would like to preserve the handmade pottery traditions of Thimi, the quality and aesthetic of ceramic goods created by hand on the potter's wheel cannot be matched by machine-produced wares. The rhythmic and delicate lines left by the potter's fingers as he pulls the clay up to form a bowl, and the soft feel of a hand-pulled cup handle that melds with the curve of one's fingers while holding the cup, give a subtle feeling of delight to the user. This is a feeling that is lost with the daily use of machine-made, mass-produced wares. As industrially made ceramics slowly eclipse handmade wares in the general market, this becomes yet another way in which the public is losing touch with its traditions and culture. The dilemma faced by Thimi Ceramics and other workshops undergoing modernization was to keep the pottery craft of Thimi rooted in traditional ways of producing pottery by hand while at the same time introducing some mechanization in order to create contemporary products that appeal to a more modern aesthetic.

There are currently 14 potters producing ceramic tableware and other household items with Santa and Laxmi Kumar at the Thimi Ceramics workshop. All work is performed collectively, beginning with the digging of clay from the rice fields. Once the clay is dug, it is mixed with water and other minerals to form soft, workable clay that undergoes a further processing of sieving and drying before being thoroughly mixed in the pugmill (a machine with a large auger that mixes clay uniformly). The potters then knead the clay with their hands, measure out the desired weights for each shape they are going to make, and then form the kneaded clay into pots on the electric wheel or press it into plaster moulds. The potters at Thimi Ceramics produce all manner of household items on the wheel including, cups, bowls, plates, lamps, vases, tea- and coffeepots, as well as flowerpots. Products made from plaster

7 Potters covering a straw kiln with ash in preparation for firing.

moulds include incense-holders, foot-scrubbers, and many varieties of oval and square dishes.

All pots are then biscuit-fired[4] in the kiln to 800°C. To some of the fired pots, a glaze coat is then applied and allowed to dry before being fired a second time in the kiln. The glazes range from cream to blue, green, yellow, brown, and black and are produced from recipes that blend different kinds of mineral and metal oxide powders with water. The pots are dipped into the liquid glaze, rendering an even coating over the surface. After applying the glaze coat, the pieces are fired a second time to 1040°C for earthenware clay and 1250°C for stoneware clay.

Throughout the 1990s, Thimi Ceramics and several of the other member workshops from the Thimi Potters' Cooperative produced these glazed earthenware goods according to methods developed with the CPPN. However, the potters began to encounter problems once again, and the need for further

8 Potter forming the base of a flowerpot.

modernization became imminent. Appreciation among the general public in Nepal did not increase over time, and potters were still finding it difficult to market their new products to Nepalis. Their market was confined predominantly to tourist hotels and restaurants, and expatriate households, and even this market began to falter due to increasing civil unrest and the Maoist insurgency that crippled the country. Fewer and fewer tourists ventured to Nepal, and expatriates began to leave on account of lack of security in the country.

Aside from the waning market for these new products, the potters were developing problems with quality control and were producing goods of a somewhat lacklustre appearance. The designs lacked freshness, and the same glazes had been used for over ten years. There were also some technical issues with the ware on account of the low temperature to which the goods were fired. Locals complained that the ceramics chipped easily and leaked when liquids were kept in them. The fragility of the earthenware clay meant that the potters had to make their pots extremely thick and heavy in order to withstand daily use in the home, and this made the goods unappealing to customers. All of these factors made for an increasingly sluggish economy in Thimi, and revealed that the issues involved in keeping the ceramic-making traditions alive in the village had not been fully resolved. There was more to be done to create a vital economy in Thimi built around a modernized version of its traditional industry.

The Thimi Ceramics Stoneware Project

In 2001, Santa and Laxmi Kumar of the Thimi Ceramics workshop embarked on a new adventure in entrepreneurship

that would further change the face of ceramic production in Thimi. This initiative has offered much opportunity and hope for the village. Beginning in the late 1980s, the two brothers had several times been afforded the chance to visit a ceramics institute called Anderson Ranch Art Center in Snowmass, Colorado, USA, where they had been exposed to the latest advances in US ceramic technology. Following these visits, the brothers yearned to bring some of this advancement to their own village, in the hope that with more available technology, production in Thimi could become increasingly competitive and survive its current economic slump.

A ceramic artist by profession, I travelled in 2001 to Kathmandu with my husband for work and study, and was asked by Santa and Laxmi Kumar to join them in a project geared towards creating the first stoneware ceramics facility in Nepal. Having been exposed to stoneware production technology at Anderson Ranch, the two brothers had determined that working with stoneware clay instead of earthenware[5] would resolve many of the technical difficulties that were making their products unmarketable, such as chipping and leaking of the ware. Stoneware, being a more durable, high-fire material, would also allow the potters to produce much thinner, lighter ware that would be suitable for export and able to survive the transport abroad. Santa and Laxmi Kumar were interested in combining their vast experience in running a pottery workshop with my own expertise in stoneware technology and ceramic design to forge a relationship that became, with the help of some grant funding from a US foundation called the Ramsay Merriam Fund, the Thimi Ceramics Stoneware Project.

The objective behind the Stoneware Project was to create

9 Potter glazing the inside of a pitcher.

new, high-quality handmade wares using a combination of modern and traditional methods. We all felt that the traditional industry in Thimi could be preserved in some form while creating new ceramic products that would be competitive in an export market. We aimed to design and produce simple, contemporary, artisan-made tableware that would retain some of the flavour of Thimi's traditional culture. The grant funding allowed for the procurement of kiln bricks suitable for higher temperature firing, as well as materials that could be blended with the indigenous clay to raise the firing temperature, and the establishment of an extensive training programme to familiarize the potters with the new methods and materials. The potters learned to throw pots much more thinly and precisely and were pushed to adhere to strict quality regulations. While Santa and Laxmi Kumar were building the kilns, I worked closely with the potters and designed a range of tableware products that would be appealing to a contemporary export market, while still reflecting an aesthetic that is unique to Thimi (figure 11). The Project developed over the course of four years, and in 2005 we sent out our first shipments to stores in the US, and began supplying some goods to expatriate customers, as well as hotels and restaurants in Kathmandu. Thimi Ceramics was

10 Potter coil-forming a large jar, used for storing grain.

11 Stoneware designed by the author, drying in the sun at Thimi Ceramics.

for the first time making a unique and viable export product (though still out of reach for most local patrons), that offered potters in the village a way out of the decline they had been experiencing in recent years.

For the first time since the beginning of the CPPN in 1982, potters in Thimi were producing artisan-made works that were entirely new and exciting. Though the Stoneware Project was small and only encompassed one workshop, it was now possible to envision ceramics in Thimi as an industry that might actually draw young artisans to the craft of their ancestors. The idea of themselves as artisans involved in the production of a high-quality craft product was a fresh concept for the potters of Thimi, and inspired them to take renewed personal responsibility for the venture. In time, this development may allow the ceramic tradition to hold a place alongside what have long been considered higher art forms by Nepali culture such as bronze-casting of religious statues, thangka painting, and jewellery making. The ceramic tradition in Thimi, preserved in this new, modernized version, may one day allow Nepali culture to value the goods produced in Thimi as they value the bronze-work of Patan, or the thangkas from Kathmandu.

***

Over the course of its history, there have been many factors that have held back development of Thimi's ceramic tradition. The general economic quagmire that has plagued the country is certainly the largest of those factors. The oppression faced by Kumales as members of a lower caste is another important aspect of the problem. The nostalgic mindset of Nepali culture in its vision of cultural traditions as part of an "old way of life" that must be rigidly preserved has also contributed to the dissolution of these traditions. The use of clay pots in the Kathmandu Valley is likely to remain as long as the Hindu-Buddhist cultures remain. Many of the simple clay wares are intimately associated with Hindu-Buddhist religious rites, including death. Pottery ritual objects associated with death rites will continue unless there is a drastic change in the way Nepalis dispose of their dead or the way in which they practice their religion in the future.

In the course of ceramic development in Thimi in the past 30 years, relatively few villagers have taken the opportunity to modernize. Though this has for the most part been on account of poor economic conditions in the workshops, there has also been marked skepticism among many of the village people with regard to technological advances. There are several workshops still in existence in which a grandfather bends over the old-style wheel he turns with a long pole, all day making the flowerpots and yogurt bowls his family has been producing for generations. His sons are in Kathmandu working as taxi drivers or waiters in a restaurant, and have little interest in the traditional culture that they were born into. It is sad that contemporary culture has in many ways eclipsed the way of life that existed in Thimi for so many generations, but to cling to it so rigidly and not allow for development or change is to snuff out its existence

with increasing speed. The answer to cultural preservation in Thimi seems to lie in the adoption of a new way of viewing the ceramic tradition in the village: in an appreciation for the art form as it exists in a larger community of artistic traditions important to Nepal's history. Preservation of these traditions lies partly in maintaining their relevance to contemporary culture, and this comes about when the thread of tradition is held steadily throughout a process of modernization.

Figure Acknowledgements
All photographs by the author, except figures 4–6.

Notes
1   Gorkha is the district headquarters of the Gorkha District of Nepal, located 154 kilometres northwest of Thimi.
2   Terra sigilatta is a fine clay slip made from settling the larger particles of clay in water and siphoning off the fine slip from the top. It is used as a smooth, shiny painting material for decorating the outside of pottery, and can be coloured with various metal oxides such as iron oxide.
3   The mortar is made from a mix of cement, sand, and rice husks. The husks burn away due to heat from the firing, and leave insulating pockets of air in their absence.
4   The initial firing of raw clay in the kiln to prepare it for glazing is called "biscuit-firing" or "bisque-firing".
5   Stoneware clay, when fired to temperatures of around 1200°C or higher, is a vitrified, and very durable ceramic material. Earthenware clay, fired to a lower temperature, remains porous after firing, and is much less durable.

Part III
PERFORMANCES AND RELIGIOUS TRADITIONS

Street Theatre
The Agora where Gods and Humans Meet

Sangita Rayamajhi

I evoke the imagery of the Greek "agora" or public open space at the very beginning of this essay because the traditional theatre of Kathmandu from ancient times was a spectacular melange of faith and quotidian reality. The cosmogonic spirit that underlies the Nepali performative culture can be understood by placing two problematics together – performance and spiritual pursuit. The fact that performance was given the greatest priority in the culture shows that the people did not want to confine their gods to their reliquaries. Gods were restless to come out and join in the festivities and travel. Public space therefore became the theatre that represented heaven, earth, community, aesthetics, and hope. And the tradition continues in modern times.

Nepal's Tradition of Theatre

Nepal's street theatre has remained strongly a part of the festive tradition, a manifestation of the cultural blend of the country's rituals and dance forms and the Indic theatrical traditions. Hadigaon, although it was the heart of the ancient city of Kathmandu, is today incorporated within the urban sprawl of the Kathmandu Valley. In ancient times, this is where the gods and humans came together in the streets in divinized cycles. It is said that this ancient city celebrates more street festivals than the days in a year. Sudarshan Tiwari, in his book *The Brick and the Bull*, describes how the gods come out of the temples to intermingle with the humans and "re-enact celestial events and scenes of the past":

> Whether demons prowl the streets, giving the gods a reason to come out of their temples to save humans, or whether the gods just need to renew their relationships with celestial relatives through a regular visit, whatever the theme or reason, festivals come into play. They are grand occasions and whole settlements come alive with them.[1]

Tiwari's expression of the fusion of the divine and the mortal on the streets establishes the tradition of performance culture in urban space. To understand the performance culture of Nepal one can go back in time to see the fusion of the folk with the urban, of the agricultural with the urban, or the fusion of power and ritual in the urban setting.

Traditional street festivals have set the precedent for the street theatre of Nepal, especially in the Kathmandu Valley. This heritage of the street, as Abhi Subedi writes:

> is an important subject when we talk about the tradition of performance in Nepal Mandala because in this sphere festivity, forms and urban architecture all become part of the theatrical tradition. Street in Nepali theatrical heritage has a very long history because it is associated with travel or movement. In fact we may even put it like this – Nepali dramaturgy developed out of the street.[2]

Street festivals such as Gai Jatra, Indra Jatra, and Bisket Jatra were all performed like dramas with people dressed up in divine and demonic costumes and masks – dancing, singing, gesticulating, parading, and riding or drawing the chariots. Almost all the festivals of yore where the gods and mortals came together were performed in the precincts of temples, or on *dabali*s (little raised platforms) that were built in the courtyards of localities where houses and temples sat facing each other. When the gods were carried in palanquins and taken to or away from these temples, they were made to rest on these *dabali*s and the local people swarmed around in a myriad of colours, from each door of the neighbourhood, to worship and join in the celebrations. One such festive performance is the Ashtamatrika dance which is an integration of a variety of dramatic forms, colourful costumes, and Charya music.[3]

Those who held power were always very close to the theatre. The kings wrote plays and poetry and drew plans for theatres. Kathmandu has many such spaces that have brought the power-holders and the people together. The interest of the rulers gave theatre a certain dimension. It became purely a means of entertainment, and never could acquire a political edge.

In Nepal the proscenium theatre, even today, is limited to a certain coterie of theatre-goers and therefore has not in any way been a strong cultural force reflecting the hopes, desires, and disenchantment of the common people. In the post-World War period of the 1940s and '50s the world was still reeling from the shock of the atomic blasts capable of ending life on earth. The time was one of stress and anxiety. The America of the '60s struggled for civil rights, through demonstrations and sit-in protests. The war in Vietnam was escalating and American theatre at that time reflected a sense of anxiety, outrage, and demand for change. On the other hand, in the Nepal of the 1940s and '50s, realist plays were performed on the proscenium, an indirect impact of the colonial rule in India.

In the early 1940s, Jyapu Natak, the theatre of the indigenous people of Kathmandu, was very popular. Theirs was an open-air theatre where they mixed traditional forms with realistic theatre. Jyapu Natak drew upon myth and folktales and it was perhaps the last of such open-air theatre groups to be seen in the streets of Kathmandu for a long, long time. A mixture of folk and urban helped to provide dynamism to the vibrant culture of performance in Nepal, where the folk

1 Children dressed for the Gai Jatra, as Krishna, a cow, and an ascetic, in memory of a deceased family member, Kathmandu. Photograph: Kamal Raj Joshi.

2 A child dressed up as a cow for Gai Jatra, Kathmandu. Photograph: Bikash Rauniyar.

continued to give a unique dynamism to the culture of the valley, to its architectural constructs, art forms, theatre, music, and dance. And this rich cultural tradition helped to keep street theatre alive in Nepal.

In the beginning plays were not directly available to the common people. Bala Krishna Sama, known as the father of Nepali theatre, began the tradition of writing original plays by assimilating oriental philosophy and aesthetics with Western literary influences and philosophical thoughts and getting them performed. Gopal Prasad Rimal, Gobinda Gothale, and Bijaya Bahadur Malla wrote social plays with themes of family norms and values. These plays were considered a means of recreational pastime, open to the common people and the royal audience alike. These plays were almost always presentational as well as representational, combining reality with fiction. Sama's *Mukunda Indira* and *Mutuko Byatha* among others were the first to be performed for the royal family and the ruling Rana aristocracy as well as for the public. But the Ranas were displeased with Sama when he performed a play called *Prahlad* in which the virtuous young boy was likened to India's freedom fighter Mahatma Gandhi and the cruel father, the demonic Hiranyakashipu was portrayed as the autocrat, representing the British rulers of India or the Ranas of Nepal. The Rana

prime minister Padma Shumsher banned the play.[4] That was probably the first major play banned for political reasons as early as the mid-1940s.

An unprecedented change occurred in the '80s and onwards when theatre, especially performed by young people, directly reflected people's quest for a democratic political system and the right to live in freedom and dignity. Rituals and festivals, intermingling of fiction and reality, were no longer valid. Theatre now had a different god.

To judge any country's theatre we have to look at the pattern of people's response to it. As young people came into street theatre the pattern of response began to change. The reasons for this were several. One was that the young theatre creators had been exposed to the movements in India to use theatre, especially street theatre, for political purposes. The second reason was that theatre creators had begun looking for means to voice protest against censorship and the non-democratic mode of the regime. The third, and I think very important, factor is that life in Nepal has always been full of events that have dramatic quality. The movement for the restoration of democracy had that theatrical and performative quality. Abhi Subedi analyses the performative nature of the movement for the restoration of democracy of 1990. Writing about the politico-performative dimension of the street show he says:

> The long procession that marched towards the Narayanhiti palace on the deciding day in a quiet manner did impress the King himself who has always been a very important protagonist in the street rituals and marches. He became the audience and the marchers became the performers. Street became the theatre, the Royal Palace became the audience's place and the slogans for political change from non-party system of government to a multiparty system of government became the dramatic text. The rhythmic slogans, marching rhythms and the use of colours did evoke a sense of street theatre. The marches and demonstrations on the streets have a great theatrical value. The big march was a combination of theatre and ritual. The marches did create a new context of performance and enactment of narration. The nationalism evoked by these marches was different from the one evoked by the ritual marches. But the ritual and theatrical modes of the marches in the new context in the Nepal Mandala did show the same carnivalesque or ritualistic features as can be seen in every form of street rituals involving marches.[5]

Modern Legacies

In 1982 the playwright Ashesh Malla with his group Sarwanam inherited the legacy of the street. In other words, theatre was born again to address the specific needs of people

3 Spectators at the Gai Jatra in Durbar Square, Kathmandu. Photograph © Dinodia.

living under political oppression. There was a slow yet sure rise of emotions that no longer could be suppressed. Theatre groups from outside the capital, from Janakpur, Pokhara, and Surkhet, started gaining prominence. They were basically impacted by the type of disillusionment that had earlier influenced youth in the Western world. Thus experimental theatre came into practice, with Camus' *The Just* and Sartre's *No Exit* finding a niche in the hearts of the people. These plays were translated into Nepali and performed. There were various other theatre groups outside the valley, like the ones in Pokhara – Pratibimba and Nava Pratibha Natyashala. (In fact, plays had been performed in Pokhara on a regular basis since 1938, initiated by the Rana general Dhana Shumsher when he was the Governor General of Pokhara.)

Saru Bhakta, a Pokhara-based playwright who basically draws his themes from myth and folklore, wrote a play to herald the arrival of democracy, *Jasto Dante Katha* (Like a Folk Tale). It was directed by Anup Baral. It is a story of kings and queens and princes, the lone princess being a metaphor for the much awaited democracy. This was performed in 1989–90. A few months later *Yudha Uhi Gas Chamber Bhitra* (Battle within That Very Gas Chamber), by the same playwright and director was performed.

Both the proscenium theatre and the street theatre belong to the people, but in Nepal where the number of proscenium theatres and the circle of theatre-goers are very limited, street theatre with its conditions of performance – the intimacy of

actors and spectators, the accessibility to diverse masses and the media – immediately captured the imagination of both playwrights and performers. This increasing interest was precipitated by the political "performance" rampant in the country. Though it is not right to brand all street plays as complete political advertisements, the street theatre people of Nepal themselves claim that their plays were entirely politically oriented. In an interview, Ashesh Malla said, "Our plays were always entirely against the government, against the Panchayat System."[6] Most of Ashesh Malla's plays are written for street theatre but some are also performed on the proscenium, for example *Mrityu Utsab* (Death Festival). But wherever performed, the plays and the hopes raised and reflected the rebellion they expressed, became a drama of disillusionment with the current political system.

The linear development of street theatre shows how the themes are basically very, very political. Street theatre heightened in popularity even as the people's desire for democracy increased. Much before Ashesh Malla had formed Sarwanam, some Nepali university students decided to challenge the existing tradition of theatre with the street play *Murdabaad ma Utheka Haathharu* (Hands Raised in Protest). Then again in 1982 two plays, *Hami Basanta Khoji Rahechaun* (We are Searching for Spring) and *Samapta Asamapta* (End Unend), were taken to the streets – the Coronation Garden within the Tribhuvan University grounds. For all these plays the street had now become a political space. In them one could

4 Veneration of Swet Bhairava at Durbar Square, Kathmandu, during the Indra Jatra. The metal-plated head was donated by Rana Bahadur Shah for the Indra Jatra in 1795. Photograph © Dinodia.

5 Crowds at the Bisket Jatra, Bhaktapur. Photograph © Thomas L. Kelly.

6 (opposite) Artist and audience mingle during a religious street theatre performance in Kathmandu Valley. Photograph © Dinodia.

7 Street theatre with a social mesage by the Sarwanam group, organized by Ashesh Malla. Photograph courtesy Sarwanam.

read a sense of rebellion, a desire to freely express oneself, a hope for democracy.

The 30-minute street play *Death Festival* (January 2001) by Ashesh Malla portrays the trauma of the Nepali people. It delineates the ever-increasing poverty of Nepali society, poverty of the minds of the politicians who "use" the common people to further their goals, their so-called ideologies in these "democratic" times. The play also portrays the People's Movement or the Maoist insurgency and how the general populace is sandwiched between corrupt politicians and brutal rebels. The politicians use the poverty and helplessness of the people to siphon away the country's money into their own hands. So these politicians, these people who had once fought for democracy, are now like Orwell's animals: "Some are more equal than others." They will suck the people dead: "You are a Nepali, you have no way out but to die of hunger and conflict." And yet again those very voices ask: "If you die who will we bring forward to show the donors the proof of our poverty?" This play is a far cry from *Hami Basanta Khoji Rahechaun*, or even from *Sesh Yudha/Yudha Ajhai Banki Cha* (The Remaining Battle/The Battle Still Remains). The angst of the people, the disillusionment, the crisis of the country reaches its climax when the politician-actor bursts out laughing, "…I am the ruler of corpses, the emperor of the dead, king of a dead city…."

Then on January 29, 2006, the street play *Bhitta* (Wall) was performed by Arohan, at a time when Nepal was in the midst of its ten-year State-Maoist war. Twenty-five blind characters shuffle around holding onto a long rope. They must stay together and keep moving. If they leave hold of the rope, they fall into the hands of the waiting police and military. Many succumb to this fate; others, by working together to overcome or outsmart the authorities, manage to escape. Those who stay together and take risks are "saved" and will hopefully return to help the others. In early 2007 and 2008, Sarwanam dramatized on the streets of Kathmandu and in 60 other districts of Nepal the play *Naya Adhyaya* (New Chapter). This street play captures

the sensitivity of the times, not just the physical conflict, but the minds of the people, especially so the dilemma of the women whose men had gone to war either on the side of the army or taken away by Maoists. These women did not stop to wallow in their condition but moved ahead, to rebel against the tyranny of fate. The drama has very little dialogue, but the performance captured the sentiments of the crowd.

If we make a longitudinal study of street theatre we find a vast shift of paradigm, a metamorphosis parallel to that suffered by the nation. Is this then a reliable picture of the history of the nation as reflected in plays? No, street theatre is not directly a mirror of changes that occur in society, but is rather a metaphor of change, reflecting the thoughts of a sensitive group of artists.

Conclusion

Street theatre, which in Nepal is the legacy of festivals, rituals, dances, colours, and costumes, dramatically evolved into a celebration of political expression. Almost any day, if you walk into Hadigaon you are certain to meet with gods and humans riding the palanquins, even today. The streets will still be alive with colours and sounds, but added to it all will now be another story, of pain and despair, of a reality different from the dream one dared to dream. The street as the agora continues to govern the life of the people of this country. Now it has become a space where dramas of extreme intensities are performed in turn or simultaneously. Streets choked by demonstrations and shuffling feet still retain the legacy of a calmer side of the culture of street plays. When the streets are clear of noisy demonstrations, deities emerge in palanquins carried by people. The ancient sounds of drums, cymbals, and flutes fill the air. Street theatre therefore continues to govern the rhythm of life of the nation through the work of contemporary theatre practitioners. The legacy of the agora of gods and humans endures in different avatars in the street theatre of Nepal.

Notes

1 Sudarshan Raj Tiwari, *The Brick and the Bull: An account of Handigaun, the ancient capital of Nepal* (Kathmandu: Himal Books, 2002), p. 10.

2 Abhi Subedi, N*epali Theatre as I See It* (Kathmandu: Gurukul School of Theatre, 2006), p. 45.

3 Tulasi Diwasa, "The Living Tradition of the *Astamatrika* Dance Drama in the Kathmandu Valley, Nepal", in *International Symposium on the Conservation and Restoration of Cultural Property* (Tokyo: Tokyo National Research Institute of Cultural Properties, 1987), p. 52. For more on Charya Nritya see the essay by Miranda Shaw in this volume.

4 Prachanda Malla, *Nepali Rangamancha* (Nepali Theatre), (Kathmandu: Royal Nepal Academy, 1980), pp. 77–78.

5 Abhi Subedi, "Travel as Theatre in Nepal Mandala", *Mandala-4* (publication of the Nepal Centre of ITI, April 2002).

6 Interview with this writer, May 2003.

Tantric Buddhist Dance of Nepal
From the Temple to the Stage and Back

Miranda Shaw

Practitioners of sacred art traditions across the globe face the challenge of preserving and adapting their cultural heritage in the face of assaults on their time-honoured ways by modern institutions and ideologies. Sacred arts that were once the preserve of well-defined communities, serving for them as vehicles of meaning and identity, are endangered by a range of forces that constitute modernity: population migrations, shifting local and transnational economies, global tourism, and new technologies for the transfer of ideas and cultural property. At the current pace of change, gradual adaptation is no longer a luxury. Many sacred art traditions have been brought to the brink of extinction by social and economic erosions of the priestly role, the rise of anti-religious political movements, the ease of mechanical reproduction, and pressures on local traditions to "globalize or perish".

One imperilled sacred art that is making the transition to modernity through new channels of transmission and performance is the tantric dance of the Buddhist priests of Nepal. They call their dance form Charya Nritya, meaning "dance as a spiritual discipline". Charya dance is also known in Newar as Chacha Pyakhan. The practitioners of this religious art are the Newar tantric priests – both male and female – of the Kathmandu Valley, known by the caste name Vajracharya, which means "master of Vajrayana". Ethnically, they are indigenous Newars rather than Nepalis, who descend from later Hindu arrivals to the valley. Vajracharya priests perform life-cycle rituals for their temple parishioners and preside over tantric initiations, feasts, and other rites. Dance is an integral part of their priestly methodology and tantric practice.

After introducing Charya dance as traditionally conceived and practised, I will trace its movement from the temple to the stage, addressing the motives of the Vajracharyas who revealed their secret art and the performing arts community that embraced it. Following consideration of the implications of this process for the content and form of the dance, I comment on its revival in a new temple setting, the first Newar Buddhist temple to be built in the West. Here, Charya dance enters a new phase with a renewed authenticity that is made possible by navigating the selfsame global crosscurrents that typify modernity.

Charya Dance as Sacred Art

The Vajracharyas trace the origins of Charya Nritya to their 10th-century founder, Shantikaracharya. The tantric master had a vision of Manjushri, the bodhisatva of wisdom, and composed a dance to commemorate the form in which the deity appeared to him. This, the first Charya dance on historical record, honoured Manjushri for his role in the creation of the Kathmandu Valley. When the area was submerged beneath a lotus lake, Manjushri journeyed to the region from his holy mountain in Tibet and saw that if the lake were drained, the place would be ideal for habitation. He danced and raised his sword, then sliced a gorge that released the waters. Swayambhu Stupa miraculously arose on a hilltop above the newly created valley. A painting on this theme by Prem Man Chitrakar features a dancing Manjushri

1 *Dancing Manjushri*, by Prem Man Chitrakar, Patan, last decade of 20th century. Pigment and gold on cloth. This contemporary painting portrays a multi-armed, golden Manjushri dancing as he creates the Kathmandu Valley, preparing the area for human habitation. Photograph: Miranda Shaw.

2 Ratna Kaji Vajracharya teaches a young Newar girl the *mudra*s of the goddess Tara. The girl wears the ornaments and flowered crown of the goddess she will represent in dance. Photograph courtesy Prajwal Ratna Vajracharya.

raising his rock-sundering sword of wisdom. Swayambhu towers on its rocky promontory in the background (figure 1).

One of the divine patrons of Charya Nritya is a dancing form of Avalokiteshvara known as Padmanarteshvara, "Lord Who Dances on a Lotus". Ritual initiation into the dance practice is a ceremony centring on Padmanarteshvara. Before commencing to dance on a given occasion, the dancer prays, recites mantras, and visualizes Padmanarteshvara to invoke the spirit of the dancing bodhisatva.

The Charya Nritya repertoire includes dances of offering, devotion, and celebration, but the primary role of the dance is to support the practice of deity yoga, a form of meditation in which one visualizes oneself as a deity in order to awaken enlightened qualities within. Dancing as the deity makes the appearance, ornaments, and qualities of the deity vividly concrete as they are translated into bodily movements.

Charya Nritya is an intricate dance style that requires immense physical and spiritual discipline. The training imparts an extensive movement vocabulary that features precise hand gestures or *mudra*s (figure 2). Many *mudra*s carry the same meaning they have in other artistic media, such as those of dispelling fear (*abhaya*) and bestowing divine blessings (*varada*) (figure 3). Others were developed specifically for the dance, such as the donning of a crown (figure 4) and speaking with a divine voice (figure 5). The movement training is supplemented by the study of iconography, philosophy, and ritual. The development of mindfulness, mastery of the mind and emotions, and cultivation of compassion, equanimity, and selflessness foster the qualities that infuse the dance with its spiritual content.

The tenor of the movements expresses the mood and awareness of the deity being represented. A meditating Buddha is the portrait of contemplative calm. Peaceful bodhisatvas appear to float through space with gentle, flowing movements and beneficent smiles (figure 6). Wrathful deities and protectors

stomp and leap with taut muscles, flailing tongues, and bared teeth (figure 7). Tantric Buddhas pulsate with yogic power and gaze, wide-eyed, with penetrating awareness (figure 8). The dancer periodically pauses in a pose that characterizes the deity in other artistic media (compare figures 8 and 9). Charya dance is ultimately a yogic art of transformation. Its performance makes the deities tangibly present in ritual settings.

Out of the Temple, Onto the Stage

For over a thousand years, practice of this secret tradition was restricted to those of Vajracharya lineage. Some dances could be viewed by their patrons in select religious settings, while others could not be witnessed outside the circle of full tantric initiates. The dance was not publicly performed until 1956, when two prominent priests, Sanu Kaji Vajracharya and Chini Kaji Vajracharya, made the controversial decision to exhibit the dance at a World Buddhist Conference in Kathmandu. Subsequently, a cohort of priests began to teach the dance to those outside their ranks. This broader exposure has gained such momentum that currently a range of Charya dances are regularly on public view in Nepal. They are incorporated into musical dramas and included in cultural festivals, dance contests, and other staged events variously produced for local audiences, visiting dignitaries, and tourists.

These secular performance venues have entailed changes in musical accompaniment, attention to staging, and more elaborate costuming. Moreover, in these settings, the Vajracharya origin of Charya dance is rarely mentioned, and the term "Charya Nritya" has given way to its designation as "classical dance" or "Nepali classical dance." This nomenclature is misleading insofar as it classifies the dance as a performing art rather than a religious practice. It also casts the dance as the cultural property of Nepal collectively rather than of a specific ethnic and religious minority.

Although these shifts in performance settings and designation would seem to represent a misappropriation of the sacred dance heritage of the Vajracharyas, the public exposure and access to the dance could not have taken place without their cooperation. Members within the Vajracharya ranks, too, had a hand in its recognition as a "classical" art.

Transmission to the Performing Arts Community

The Vajracharya priests centrally responsible for disseminating Charya dance to the performing arts community were the late Sapta Muni and Ratna Kaji, beginning in the 1970s. Priests Asha Kaji and Kancha Buddha also played a role. My reconstruction of the transmission process here draws primarily on my interviews of key actors in this process: Ratna Kaji Vajracharya, his son Prajwal Ratna Vajracharya, Rajendra Shrestha, and Yagya Man Shakya, whose respective roles are discussed in what follows.

One major line of transmission can be traced through the National Theatre, or Rashtriya Nachaghar, which means,

3 Prajwal Ratna Vajracharya dancing as the bodhisatva of compassion, displays the *mudra* that dispels fear with his right hand and the *mudra* of divine generosity with his left. Photograph: Terry Wilson.

literally, "national" (*rashtriya*) "house" (*ghar*) of "dance" (*nacha*). Dance and drama are closely intertwined in Nepal, for dramatic productions typically incorporate dance, and thus dance training is integral to theatrical education. Sapta Muni Vajracharya was the first to transmit Charya dance to the dance troupes of Nepal through a teaching career at the National Theatre that spanned the 1970s through to 1992 or 1993, when he passed away. His students went on to teach Charya dance at high schools and colleges and to their private students and troupes.

The dances taught by Sapta Muni still form the mainstay of the Charya repertory that is performed on the stage by non-Vajracharyas. The esoteric dance of the female Buddha Vajrayogini (see figure 8), formerly performed only in rituals attended by full tantric initiates, became the centrepiece of the public Charya repertoire. Sapta Muni also taught the dances of Manjushri (see figures 5 and 6) and of the five transcendent Buddhas (Pancha Buddha). Sapta Muni created Tara and Bala Kumari dances for the theatre, as well as one devoted to the Hindu deity couple Bhairava and Kali.

Kancha Buddha Vajracharya taught Charya dance at the

National Theatre after Sapta Muni passed away and added several dances to the curriculum, among which only that of White Ganesha (figure 10) today holds a recurrent spot in public performances.

Asha Kaji Vajracharya and Ratna Kaji Vajracharya participated in the transmission process through private instruction of non-Vajracharyas. Asha Kaji steadfastly limited his teaching to his countrymen, while Ratna Kaji accepted a select number of students from the United States, Europe, Japan, and Australia in the late 1970s and early '80s. Thereafter, he directed such students to study with Rajendra Shrestha and, beginning in the early '90s, with his own son Prajwal Ratna. Some of these international students now teach and perform the dances in their home countries.

Rajendra Shrestha is another important figure in the transfer of Charya Nritya from the temple to the stage. The young Rajendra, as an early student of Sapta Muni at the National Theatre, was drawn to the beauty and spirituality of Charya dance and began performing it in 1975. After his theatre apprenticeship, Rajendra became a private student of Asha Kaji and Ratna Kaji. Although not a Buddhist by birth, Rajendra dedicated himself to the promotion of Charya Nritya and began in 1981 to create an organization for that purpose. In 1985, he joined with guru Ratna Kaji and singer Kamal Chettri to formally launch Kala Mandapa: Institute of Nepali Classical Performing Arts. Rajendra took the helm as acting instructor,

4 Prajwal Ratna Vajracharya makes the gesture of donning a crown of wisdom. This image beautifully captures the precision and fluid grace of the movement. Photograph: Terry Wilson.

5 A young Prajwal Ratna Vajracharya, dancing as Manjushri in a temple courtyard, signals that the deity has a single face and speaks with a divine voice that delights and illuminates all beings. Photograph courtesy Prajwal Ratna Vajracharya.

teaching and staging regular performances at the Hotel Vajra in Kathmandu, which he does to the present day as the hotel's resident artist. After offering classes to tourists for almost two decades, Rajendra now devotes his teaching and directing efforts to a small troupe of young Nepalis and Newars.

Rajendra developed the theatrical aspect of Charya dance for public performance by introducing new modes of musical accompaniment, establishing methods for travelling across a stage, and enhancing the costuming. He also created a stable niche and physical home for Charya dance as a performing art during the decades when it was gaining a foothold in public awareness.

Another student of Sapta Muni who became a prominent teacher and performer of Charya dance is Yagya Man Shakya, who held the distinguished post of Director of the National Theatre from 2001 to 2009. Yagya Man gained admission to the theatre in 1985, where he studied Charya dance with Sapta Muni for seven or eight years and then with Kancha Buddha for several more. In adulthood, Yagya Man learned additional Charya dances from Sangeeta Shrestha, another theatre graduate who teaches Charya dance at Padma Kanya

Campus. Yagya Man was the featured dancer at the 250th Kumari Jatra Anniversary and Celebration of World Tourism Day cultural programme in 2007, which included folk and Charya dances. Yagya Man performed the dances of Vajrayogini and White Ganesha (see figure 10) and the Bhairava role in the Bhairava-Kali dance.

Charya dance has special meaning for Yagya Man as both an indigenous and a Buddhist art form. He produced a play about the origins of the Kathmandu Valley, *Naga Dahe* (Naga Lake), using the Manjushri dance as the point of departure for a full-length dance drama, available on a DVD of the same name. Eager to expand his repertoire, he is setting dances to the Charya songs published in a 1986 booklet by Kala Mandapa. Yagya Man would love to undertake further study, but such training is not currently available. At present, no Vajracharyas residing in Nepal are willing to admit outsiders to their ranks, even one such as Yagya Man, a Newar Buddhist of the Shakya caste (some of whom claim descent from Buddha Shakyamuni) who can view the dances in ritual settings.

6 Prajwal Ratna Vajracharya, dancing as a peaceful bodhisatva, raises his hands in the gesture of reassurance for all living beings in the universe. Photograph: André Elbing.

7 Wrathful deities and protectors are characterized by taut muscles and intense, often dramatic movements. The costume, as worn here by Prajwal Ratna Vajracharya, features a "tigerskin" skirt and "skull" necklace. Photograph courtesy Prajwal Ratna Vajracharya.

Vajracharya Motivations for Revelation of the Dance

The revelation of Charya Nritya outside of its tantric ritual context was prompted by several factors. One was the political repression of education and the arts and specific bans on Vajracharya ritual during the period of Rana rule that ended in 1951. The new government under the Shah rulers restored funding of the arts and education, established the Royal Nepal Academy in 1957, and lifted bans on Vajracharya practices. This background frames the decision to showcase Charya dance at the World Buddhist Conference in 1957. After decades of severe cultural repression, some Vajracharyas wanted to assert their possession of a rich and valuable tradition. Yagya Man attributes Sapta Muni's teaching career to the same motivation: "He wanted to show others, 'We have this dance . . . we have this kind of culture and dance.'" Thus, some Vajracharyas publicly revealed their secret dance in order to gain wider recognition of their unique cultural legacy and thus to promote its survival.

Ratna Kaji Vajracharya explained to me that another reason for the revelation of Charya dance to non-Vajracharyas was a concern that the hereditary transmission system no longer assured its preservation. Decreasing numbers of younger Vajracharyas devote themselves to the priestly role or aspire to become fulltime priests, in large part because they cannot support themselves on the meagre voluntary donations they receive for their time-consuming ritual ministrations. Because the number of young persons learning the dance was quite small, the tradition hung by a tenuous thread in the 1970s and '80s. Thus, Ratna Kaji and others responded to this predicament of modernity by creating alternative modes of transmission. They recognized that an existing tradition can evolve and be reinvested with traditional meanings, while an extinct tradition cannot.

The decision to reveal the dance to non-Vajracharya audiences, students, and scholars such as myself remains controversial. Senior priests Manju Vajra Vajracharya, Sapta Vajra Vajracharya, and Badri Ratna Vajracharya have vocally opposed this trend. Badri Ratna, a highly revered guru, has publicly denounced Ratna Kaji and his son Prajwal Ratna over the last two decades for "selling our secrets for money". Interestingly, however, Badri Ratna recently conceded, in August of 2008, that Vajracharya mantras – which are vastly more secret than the dances – should be publicly revealed and recorded for the sake of their preservation. It will be interesting to see whether Badri Ratna revises his stance on the revelation of the dance now that he, too, has recognized the pressing need for preservation at the sacrifice of secrecy.

Embrace by the Performing Arts Community

Yagya Man Shakya helped me understand that the performing arts community has embraced Charya dance as a genre that the people of Nepal can claim as their own. He is careful not to say "this is *our* dance"; rather, he says, "this is from Nepal". He readily admits that, as a Shakya, he would not have been able to learn Charya Nritya in former times and still cannot learn some dances that are held in secrecy. Asked whether he has any misgivings about performing a religious dance on the public stage, Yagya Man underscored that Charya dance is not entertainment; rather, it has religious meaning as a dance style devoted to "the gods and goddesses":

> Whoever knows the language, mudras, and words are very interested to see those dances. Bharat Natyam, Kathak, and Kathakali are from India. Charya is from Nepal. When I present it on stage, I'm feeling, "this is from Nepal". The folk dances are only for entertainment, but when I do Charya, I'm feeling, "this is from Nepal", so I'm very serious. Everyone who dances Charya must be like that – very serious.

For artists such as Yagya Man, then, adopting Charya as a "classical dance" is an expression of national pride. The performance of Charya Nritya also serves for him, as a Newar Buddhist, albeit not a Vajracharya, as an assertion of Buddhist identity. It is moreover clear that he derives special satisfaction from the practice of an artistic genre with a devotional dimension.

Results of Movement to the Stage

The movement of Charya Nritya to the stage and its acceptance as a classical art – the shared cultural heritage of the people of Nepal – has brought heightened attention to the dance and attracted a new generation of performers. This will inarguably help to preserve the dance during the transition to modernity. There is also, however, an attendant dilution of content and form.

When students learn such dance with the primary aim of stage performance, the meditative, ritual, and yogic elements integral to its traditional practice are diminished. The central purpose of the dance as a spiritual discipline and ritual art is not present, regardless of the sincerity and seriousness a given dancer brings to its study and performance. Religious initiations and teachings that would accompany traditional instruction are not available, and therefore the deeper content of the dance practice is compromised in the course of its public transmission.

The form of the dance, too, loses nuance and precision. The spiritual content and meaning of a given Charya dance guide the execution of its form. For example, dancing the dance of Avalokiteshvara, the bodhisatva of compassion, with the requisite gentleness, fluidity, and expression of peace (see figures 3 and 4) requires ongoing dedication to the practice of compassion in daily life. Capturing the intense, blissful gaze of Vajrayogini (see figure 8) requires a grounding in the meditative practices that yield experiential access to her powerful presence. Therefore, the form of the dance inevitably suffers to the degree that its content is de-emphasized.

8 Prajwal Ratna Vajracharya adopts a characteristic stance of Vajrayogini as she wields a crescent-shaped knife in her right hand and raises a bowl of nectar with her left. Photograph: Miranda Shaw.

9 *Vajrayogini*, by Amrit Karmacharya of Patan, last decade of 20th century. Pigment and gold on cloth. Comparison of this painting with figure 8 demonstrates the convergence between dance movements and artistic representations of the deities in other media. Photograph: Miranda Shaw.

10 Yagya Man Shakya dancing as White Ganesha at a cultural programme staged for tourists during the 2007 Kumari Jatra. Yagya Man has innovated by substituting face make-up for the traditional Ganesha mask. Photograph: Dina Bangdel.

Back to the Temple

In response in part to the dilution of the tradition and importation of Hindu elements in the public performance arena, Ratna Kaji's youngest son, Prajwal Ratna Vajracharya, formed Dance Mandal: Foundation of Classical Performing Arts in Kathmandu in 1996. Dance Mandal is dedicated to the preservation of the sacred intent and content of the dance form, and is reviving the traditional vocal accompaniment. Prajwal has toured North America, Europe, and Asia as a solo performer and with his company, performing and staging workshops, bringing his unique Buddhist heritage onto the world stage. He relocated to the USA in 2000 and now lives in Portland, Oregon, where he teaches Charya dance and performs rituals, such as marriages and house purification ceremonies, for Newars in the area.

Most relevant for the present discussion, Prajwal has established a Newar temple in Portland in collaboration with his student of five years, Helen Appell, who also teaches and performs with him. Initially his students were those for whom Charya dance was their first introduction to Buddhist teachings and meditation. For several years, though, Prajwal

has increasingly attracted serious practitioners of Tibetan and Zen Buddhism who see the dance as a way to augment and deepen their Dharma practice.

The recently completed temple in Portland, Nritya Mandala Mahavihar, was consecrated in November of 2009 and can now serve as a permanent home for Charya Nritya and other Newar practices in the West.[1] Prajwal's approach to teaching features the spiritual practices related to Charya dance. Each two-hour class includes a Dharma talk and a meditation or ritual practice as well as dance instruction. The Padmanarteshvara initiation is offered to those who study for at least a year and demonstrate a sufficient level of seriousness and commitment to continue the practice.

Thus, Charya dance has moved from the temple to the stage and back. This "return" to the temple, however, has entailed the creation of a new kind of temple space in a different cultural context. In Nepal, political upheaval and Marxist assaults on religion have placed Buddhist culture and institutions once again in peril. The Newar temple in Portland could well provide a platform for the return of authentic Charya dance to the temples of Nepal. Prajwal returns to Kathmandu periodically to teach his students there, and is increasingly approached by young Vajracharyas who want to learn this aspect of their tradition precisely because they have encountered it in public venues and thereby come to recognize its worth. The international interest in Charya Nritya, too, has fostered renewed appreciation for the art in its community of origin.

Thus, the national exposure and international migration of Charya Nritya could well prove to be the grounds of its revival in Nepal. The resurrection of the local – local art, practice, and identity – as a direct result of globalization is a dynamic of modernity that plays out in many communities across the world today. Public performance of sacred traditions, the interest of cultural tourists, and the appreciation of a global audience become, paradoxically, the conditions for the revival of imperilled local cultural traditions.

Note

1 Prajwal has produced a documentary video, *Charya Nritya: Tantric Buddhist Dance of Nepal*, available on the website, www.dancemandal.com, which also provides photographs, a schedule of programmes, and reports on progress on the temple.

Celebrating Shiva at Pashupati

Tim Ward

Once a year, hundreds of grey-bearded sadhus, babas, gurus, yogis, and other varieties of holy men come from all over India and Nepal to the Pashupati temple on the outskirts of Kathmandu, near the airport. They arrive in late February or early March to celebrate Shivaratri, the day of Shiva's birth. Like Prayag (Allahabad) in India during the Kumbh Mela, Shivaratri is a major event for holy men throughout the Hindu world, especially followers of Shiva. How do they demonstrate their devotion? By smoking copious amounts of *ganja*. Although hashish is illegal in Nepal, charitable organizations set up distribution centres on the outskirts of the temple and dole it out free of charge to the holy men during the holiday. As a writer of three books on Asian culture and religion, I explain Shivaratri to my North American friends like this: "It's like Christmas – the birth of God – but with hundreds of Santa Clauses going to the Vatican and getting stoned."

The festival lasts for a week, and I was fortunate to be back in Nepal on a brief assignment at that time.[1] I did my work during the day, then each evening slipped down to the temple grounds where the crowds were gathering. The excitement built up to the day of Shivaratri itself, when it seemed that everyone in Kathmandu came to Pashupati to worship. The temple grew so packed that more than 1,000 police were on duty for crowd control before dawn. I woke up at 6 in the morning, something I don't do at home on a regular basis. The queue to the temple was already backed up to the front door of my hotel, Dwarika's, a good kilometre and a half from the entrance to the main temple. It would take these devotees six hours to make it inside to deliver their offerings and receive their blessings, but everyone waited patiently. They seemed excited and cheerful, even in the early morning darkness.

Fortunately I had made friends with a young Nepali named Aristu who had a festival grounds pass. He had been helping his mother, who was working at one of the guru tents inside Pashupati all week. The pass allowed us to sidestep the queue and walk straight to the entrance to the temple grounds. We were not really jumping the queue since I was not lining up to enter the holiest of holies – only Hindus are allowed inside the inner courtyard. Aristu flashed a pass at armed guards, and we slipped inside the grounds.

I had met Aristu a few days earlier on the forested, shrine-studded hilltop that rises next to Pashupati. He was a 19-year-old biochemistry student, the same age as my own son back in America. He told me that his whole family had become quite religious recently. They all venerated his mother's guru and practised yoga. As a student of science, he himself believed "only 50-50". Keen to practise his English, he offered to be my guide for Shivaratri. Aristu lived amid the rice fields on the far side of Pashupati, a rural area rapidly disappearing as new homes and paved roads filled the valley. "My father tells me that 20 years ago, here at night one could often hear the cry of the wolf," he said. Soon the temple grounds will be surrounded by the city on three sides, with its back against a golf course and the airport.

Half the hilltop has been preserved as a forest behind a tall iron fence. Some 300 tiny deer race through the trees. Aristu told me the park was created in honour of Shiva, since according to the legend (from *Nepalamahatmya*) Shiva came to this hilltop ages ago in order to escape the wearying company of the gods at Banaras. He disguised himself as a golden deer and joined the local herd. His wife, Parvati, knowing his identity, joined him secretly in the form of a doe. As Hindu literature coyly describes it, the divine couple "frolicked" here for some time until the other gods tracked them down. In the scuffle to retrieve the recalcitrant Shiva, they seized him by the shining horn on his head and it broke into pieces.[2] One of the pieces took the shape of a linga and was buried at the spot where the main temple stands today. On it, four faces of Shiva as Pashupati have been carved. This is the statue that all the people of Kathmandu come to worship on Shivaratri.

Tradition says that the linga was discovered where the temple now stands when a cowherd found his cow repeatedly dripping her milk onto a certain spot. The local villagers dug up the spot, and uncovered the sacred phallus. The first shrine was supposedly built on the site in the 3rd century CE; however, historical records indicate it was rebuilt with a golden roof by King Shiva Deva III (r. 1099–1126). An earlier inscription from 605 declares that King Amshuvarman was favoured by his touching of Pashupati's feet. This gives historical legitimacy to the idea that Pashupati may have been the tutelary god of the rulers of the Kathmandu Valley from ancient times.[3]

The name Pashupati means "Lord of the Animals"; it is Shiva's earliest manifestation, and remains one of his most important throughout the Hindu world. Seals and vessels from the prehistoric Indus Culture (4500–1900 BCE) depict Pashupati(?) as a cross-legged, horned god with matted hair and erect phallus, flanked by beasts and serpents, who is generally identified with the later divinity Shiva. This prehistoric version of Pashupati is believed to be connected with nascent forms of yoga as well. According to early scriptural references, the first followers of Pashupati were yogis – long-haired, god-intoxicated ascetics who covered their bodies with ash.

In the 2nd century BCE, a formal Pashupata sect took shape. It was founded by the ascetic Lakulisha, who supposedly died while performing harsh austerities. Shiva entered his resurrected corpse and Lakulisha became a leader of the ascetic devotees of the god. He founded a "City of Shiva" that drew more than 10,000 yogis, and forged them into a cohesive sect that endured for over 2,000 years. At the heart of the sect was the notion that human civilization covered up the true nondual nature of reality; their yogic practices thus sought to free individuals from all social conventions. They let their hair and nails grow to stupendous lengths; they covered their bodies in ash, wore tigerskins, or went completely naked. Some even masturbated in public. They became known as the Order of Lunatics.

1 Pashupati temple. Photograph © Thomas L. Kelly.

2 Shiva temple with iron trident at Pashupati. Photograph: Tim Ward.

3–9 Sadhus of various sects at Pashupati. Photographs: Tim Ward.

As centuries passed, the Pashupata yogis evolved into three subsects. The Kalamukhas, named for the black streak across their face that marked their death and renunciation, were the mildest sect, since they also practised moral virtues. The Kapalikas abandoned all social and moral codes. They carried a bowl made from a human skull from which they ate and drank. They lived in cemeteries among the dead. Most extreme of all, the Aghoris, the "nonterrible", deliberately violated social taboos. They covered themselves in filth, slept on garbage, ate their own excrement and even the flesh of corpses.[4] "The process is a ruthless one," one scholar states about the path of the Pashupata sects:

> It requires the individual to abandon all these things which men most cherish, and to strip, layer by layer, the veils of ignorance, conditioning, and delusions which separate his awareness from the immortal soul. True insight and inspiration, a new awakened sense of magic and wonder is the start of the journey to the Eternal. Without this, it is not possible to escape from the world of relativity.[5]

Before dawn, Aristu and I entered the temple grounds, still a kilometre from the temple, but crushed by the crowd. Strands of tiny, bright, multicoloured lights (Christmas lights, I would call them) twinkled along the fences and treetops. For an hour we shuffled forward in the dark like some massive zombie army. As we neared the main temple, Aristu flashed his badge once more. We hopped a few cords, left the line to the temple, and found ourselves for the first time in open space. As dawn broke, we crossed the bridge over the Bagmati river. The ghats leading down to the water's edge blazed with cremation pyres. So many people receive their last rites here that the river is clogged with the silt of ashes. All week I watched workmen, kneedeep, shovelling out the accumulated sludge, trying to get a bit of a flow back into the river. Prolonged drought had turned it into a fetid trickle that dribbles through the city. The Bagmati picks up more sewage and trash than it does water. You know when you are near a bridge in Kathmandu – it stinks. You have to hold a scarf or a sleeve to cover your face in order to breathe.

On the far bank of the Bagmati, we climbed the stairs up the hill to a viewpoint overlooking the golden-roofed pagoda in which the four-faced linga rests. Around the shrines and

10 Ash-smeared sadhus at Pashupati. Photograph: Teresa Erickson.

stairways the holy men had made their camps. Tiny, smoky fires glowed orange before the makeshift altars of talismans and icons. Iron *trishula*s (tridents, the sacred weapon of Shiva), were planted firmly in the ground around the camps. The men cupped their hands and sucked the sweet smoke from their *chillim*s (chillum pipes), chanting and chatting with their comrades and curious onlookers. A haze of *ganja* hung blue in the morning air. Teenage boys seemed keen to join in the sacred act, though Aristu said he had no intention of getting high.

I was riveted by the human artwork, how each sadhu marks himself with ash and paint – vermilion and bright yellow triangles on the forehead, or stark white lines. Some have let their hair grow long and wild: moustaches curled at the ends or drooped over the mouth like that of a walrus, dreadlocks coiled round and round the head like massive frizzy turbans. They reminded me of a prehistoric cave painting come to life. Indeed, these men seem like something out of time – inhabitants not of the 21st century, but of Shiva's timeless realm.

Aristu ushered me through a door in a walled compound next to the stairs. Past a series of shrines we found more than a hundred sadhus gathered in the courtyard. My young guide pointed out to me the various types. Among the saffron-robed sadhus, we spotted ascetics who sat naked but for a loincloth, their bodies covered in ash, their hair wound around their heads in matted dreadlocks. Two men wore black robes and turbans. Aristu told me they were eaters of corpses. He said one of them lived in a hermitage in the cliffs further up the river. People were afraid of him. The more extreme of the Pashupata sects still do exist, I thought. I looked at the man. He had a grey beard, neatly trimmed. His black robe and turban were clean. He sat alone, looking down, with long iron tongs of some kind resting on one shoulder. He appeared thoughtful, self-contained. In another corner of the compound a naked man stood at the centre of a group. His dishevelled hair dangled down to his ankles. He wore dozens of strands of prayer beads around his neck that looped down and somewhat covered his genitals. I kept expecting these extreme practitioners to have the faces of maniacs. But this naked man, when he turned and I saw his face, had the sweetest, kindest expression. Although his peers seemed to honour and revere him, he seemed almost bashful, looking down, and grinning like a child at play.

To me it seemed amazing to see men like this, so out of step with modern times. But Shiva's devotees have always stepped away from their society. They were "lunatics" from the very beginning. I tried to talk to some of them but Aristu was too shy to translate. Some knew a few words of English. Some encouraged me to take their picture and then hit me up for a donation. I bought a packet of biscuits for one ragged pair who had made a pilgrimage from Bihar, which they then shared with me in easy silence. Others offered to share their *chillim*s but I declined, being too present in my own space and time.

Four months after this experience I had the fortune to visit Kathmandu again, and went to Pashupati with two journalist

11 The author with a sadhu at Pashupati. Photograph: Teresa Erickson.

friends, one of whom had studied in Banaras and written extensively about Pashupati and its holy men. With them as my interpreters, I entered the compound where the sadhus were staying. It was dusk, and a prayer ceremony was taking place on the banks of the Bagmati river. *Bhajan*s (spiritual songs) and the twang of a sitar could be heard in the night air. The music was punctuated by a band of monkeys jumping back and forth on the compound's tin roof, beating out their own cacophonous rhythms and screeching to each other now and then. About 30 holy men sat around the compound, some readying themselves for sleep, others clustered in conversation. We found a group of three sitting on a raised stone circle, willing to talk with us about their lives.

Bharati was a Naga baba, a Shiva devotee from Banaras. He had a long black beard and slender body – easy to notice from his naked chest – covered with several necklaces. He wore a large saffron turban with a huge orange *tika* (*tilak*) mark on his forehead. On his feet were white athletic socks, which may have been donated by a foreign tourist like me. My interpreters told me that though he was the youngest of the group, he was in fact the most senior baba in terms of attainment. There was, I discovered, a very clear pecking order in the world of sadhus.

Panchla Das was in his 50s, and had been a baba for twenty years. He followed the god Ram. He wore nothing but a white dhoti wrapped around his waist and a single necklace – the most minimalist decoration I had seen on a sadhu. Hanuman Baba, named after Hanuman the monkey god, was a 60-year-old Nepali farmer who had left his wife and children at age 45 to become a sadhu. Despite his Santa-like grey beard, his yellow robes, and white stripes marking his forehead, he was the junior baba of the group.

I first asked why they came to Pashupati for Shivaratri.

"It's the festival of the babas," said Panchla Das, "so lots of high-level babas come here. It's where we get to meet them and learn from them."

"Also, because the high babas come, a lot of lay people also visit, so we all benefit. It's really good for the junior babas like us," Hanuman Baba added.

"Why do you dedicate your life to God?" I asked.

They responded with a lot of chatter that I did not understand. I first thought they would have different answers, but I learned that they were in agreement. They all said that the sacred music had something to do with their decision to become a baba. Music has the power to enchant, and apparently all three babas were drawn to the devotional songs called *bhajan*s.

Panchla Das said he was 30 and married when he left his village and family. For him, the path of a sadhu was a means to get rid of bad karma that he had accumulated in this and past lives. He said his present was devoted to prayer in order to improve his future lives.

Bharati, the Naga baba, said that he was only 10 years old when he dedicated himself to Shiva. Being a sadhu was the only life he could remember.

"What's the greatest hardship being a sadhu?" I asked.

"No problems!" said Panchla Das.

"God provides everything," Hanuman Baba observed.

"Solitude is the hardest part to handle," Bharati stated.

"And what's the most beautiful thing about this life?"

Panchla Das replied, "Life itself is wonderful. Even when we are in the mountains, we never go hungry. God provides. God finds someone to support us with food or whatever we need."

"For example?"

"Tonight God sent the three of you to talk with us!" said Hanuman Baba. (This was a subtle hint that we were expected to make a donation in exchange for this conversation.) Then another sadhu named Hanuman Das wandered over to our group. He was barely five feet tall and wore a big white turban that turned out to be mostly hair. He told us he was over 100 years old. To prove it, he took off his turban and displayed his matted hair, which fell all the way to the flagstone floor. We expressed admiration for his advanced age.

"It's because we are vegetarian," the old man said, "and dedicate our lives to praying to God. That prolongs our lives. Watch this!" He grabbed his right foot and bent it up to touch the back of his ear, balancing neatly on the other foot. He looked around at the group, pleased at our astonished response. Satisfied that he had made his point, he coiled his hair back up into his turban, and wandered off into the night.

I resumed my questioning of the others: "Why do you choose to stay here, at Pashupati?"

"Because this area belongs to God. He takes care of everybody," said Panchla Das.

"And it brings people, who make donations. So God takes care of everybody," Hanuman Baba remarked.

Bharati Baba added that Pashupati is one of the 12 *pinda*s – sacred sites of Shiva. "So we come to pray here. It's also the only site with a five-faced Shiva linga in the whole world."

"Five-faced? I thought it was four-faced," I asked my journalist friends. They explained that the linga has four faces – one on each side – and one on the top facing the sky; the highest one is in abstract form.

"In our modern society life seems to move awfully fast. But you sadhus seem to have stepped out of time. What's it like for you, not to be part of this modern world?"

Bharati Baba was quick to respond, "Modern people need cell phones to talk and planes to travel. But if you meditate for 12 years, you can go into a trance and see the whole world."

"When we journalists look at the world, we see problems – political, environmental, and social. What do you see?"

After some discussion, my friend translated, "Politics and economics don't exist for us. When we see 'the world,' we see sinners, criminals, and greedy people."

"When you look to the future, what do you see?"

Panchla Das: "A lot of joy – joy in the name of Shiva."

Hanuman Baba: "We have given our lives to the devotion of Shiva. Whatever comes, we accept it in the name of Shiva."

Notes

1 I returned to Kathmandu in 2009 during Shivaratri.

2 For the origin of Pashupati, readers are referred to Daniel Wright's *History of Nepal* (1877, reprinted Kathmandu: Nepal Antiquated Book Publishers, 1972, see chapter 2). The story of Shiva and Parvati disguised as Kiranti and Kirantini sporting in the Slesmankata forest near Pashupati is also found in Pandit Viswa Raj Sharma's *Swasthani Brata Katha* (Bhairahawa, Nepal: Sarva Hiteishi Company, 1990), see chapter 14. Another major source for the study of Pashupati is Govinda Tandon's *Pashupati Kshetra ko Samskritik Adhyayana* (in Nepali), A Cultural Study of Pashupati and its Surroundings (Kathmandu: P.U. Printers, 1996).

3 For a good discussion on the origin, linga motif, and architecture of Pashupati, see Mary S. Slusser, *Nepal Mandala: A Cultural Study of the Kathmandu Valley* (Princeton, New Jersey: Princeton University Press, 1982), Vol. 1, pp. 223–34.

4 See Mark Amaru Pinkham, *The Return of the Serpents of Wisdom* (Kempton, Illinois: Adventures Unlimited Press, 1998), pp. 116–18.

5 Shri Gurudev Mahendranath, *The Yoga Vidya of Immortality* (Kathmandu: International Nath Order, 2001), p. 9.

Kumari
Caught between Past and Present

Deepak Shimkhada

The Kumari of Kathmandu is a virgin girl who is worshipped as the goddess Durga. Although the tradition of worshipping a virgin girl in the form of a goddess is quite ancient in Nepal, few had taken an interest in the subject until Michael Allen, an Australian anthropologist, studied it in the 1970s and published his findings in a book.[1] His subsequent research showed the existence of 11 such goddesses in the Kathmandu Valley.[2] In this article, I will focus on the Kumaris of Kathmandu, Patan, and Bhaktapur (figures 1–4) – the three main cities of the Kathmandu Valley – because they have been the subject as well as the object of the media, government, politicians, and human rights groups during the past few years. In particular, the Royal Kumari of Kathmandu city (figure 1) has been the subject of controversy as we will see shortly.

In order to examine this controversy, it is necessary to trace the history of Kumari, the cult of worshipping a virgin, a tradition that is headed for extinction with the collapse of the monarchy that supported it. Will the annual festival of Kumari, celebrated with much fanfare and other rituals associated with her, soon be just a memory? Or will it continue to survive, albeit with some modifications, to reflect the changing times? This article will attempt to answer these questions heuristically.[3]

The Beginnings of Kumari Worship
The idea of the worship of a pre-pubescent virgin girl as a living embodiment of the Goddess Durga is a very ancient cult among the Hindus. In fact, in the *Devimahatmya*, the bible of the followers of the goddess, Durga makes her first appearance as a nubile virgin (*kumari*) who bewitches the titans who want her to be the spouse of their leader. Indeed, in the annual Durga Puja in Bengal, it is obligatory to find at least one virgin girl who is ritually worshipped as the goddess, which is called Kumari Puja. It may also be pointed out that the name of the southern tip of India known as Cape Comorin is really Kanyakumarika which literally means the place of the virgin girl, whose antiquity goes back well over two millennia. The tradition of vestal virgins was also an important part of the worship of Athena and other Greek goddesses and the ancient Greek religion and was also known in other ancient civilizations in West Asia. However, nowhere has the cult of the Kumari remained as important, as ecumenical, and as much a vehicle of national fervour as in the small Kathmandu Valley.

The Kumari is considered a living goddess, especially in the form of the royal goddess Taleju, a form of Durga. The Royal Kumaris have been connected with the kings of Nepal for centuries. Although the worship of Kumari was officially instituted by King Jayaprakash Malla of Kathmandu in 1757 with the building of a permanent home (Kumari Ghar) for her (figures 5 and 6), Kumari's origin can be traced back at least to King Trailokya Malla of Bhaktapur in the 16th century, with the cult of Taleju (figure 7). According to one legend, it was this king who after forfeiting the right to see Durga in person, founded the worship of Kumari as a virgin girl.[4] However, Goddess Taleju, believed to have been brought to

1 The Royal Kumari of Kathmandu. Photograph: Bikash Rauniyar.

the Kathmandu Valley by King Harasimha in 1323 from Simrongarh, remained a tutelary deity of the Malla dynasty for centuries. The allusion to Kumari goes still further back. Two manuscripts dated 1280 and 1285 describe the methods of choosing, ornamenting, and worshipping a Kumari.[5]

Another entry found in a Nepali *Vamsavali* (chronicle) supports the existence of Kumari as an institution even further. According to this *Vamsavali*, King Gunakamadeva of the 12th century instituted the Indra Jatra and erected images of Kumari.[6] It is amply evident from these sources that the institution of Kumari in Nepal is an ancient one.

There are various versions of how Taleju came to occupy the body of a young girl. However, common to all is the story that the goddess was somehow offended by a Malla king and that this king was Trailokya Malla or Jayaprakash Malla, depending on which version one believes. According to legend, Goddess Taleju appeared in human form before this king, who received blessings and advice from her. The pair of them played *tripasa* (a game of dice), but at some point the ruler overstepped his authority and behaved in a sexually inappropriate manner toward the goddess. The goddess took exception to this, and she abandoned the king, promising, however, to reappear in the form of a female child, thereby forestalling the lust of any

future kings. The young female virgin goddess would not be thought of sexually, but rather a-sexually in the sense that she represented pure power, uncompromised by adult-rated longings for sexual activity.[7]

Since then, every year in September, a grand festival called Kumari Ratha Jatra is held in her honour. The reigning king would go to Kumari's residence to receive her blessings, and would be given the mandate to rule for a year. Kumari Ratha Jatra, which actually coincides with another important annual festival, Indra Jatra, signals the end of the monsoon season. The monsoon in the Kathmandu Valley brings more rain than necessary, and therefore the end of the rain is a welcome sign. And what better way to celebrate than with a festival dedicated to Indra, the God of Rain, and Kumari, the Living Goddess who brings prosperity.[8]

Prithvi Narayan Shah (1723–75), the founder of the last dynasty of modern Nepal, conquered the Kathmandu Valley in 1768/69. He continued the custom of worshipping the living goddess Kumari and accepting her as the protector of his own dynasty. Hence the tradition that had originated during the Malla period was kept alive by the Shah kings without much modification both in form and belief. So the worship of Kumari has a long history and is fundamental to Nepali culture as witnessed by the colourful Kumari Ratha Jatra celebrated every year.

From the time of the Malla kings in the 16th century to the abdication of the last Shah ruler in 2008, Kumari has played the role of protector of kings. Nepal has now assumed a new identity as a republic, but does the republic not need protection as well? Surely the adoption of a new political system does not justify abolishing age-old traditions unless they are cruel and harmful.

Harmony between Hindus and Buddhists: The Kumari Selection Process

The process of selecting a Kumari[9] has sparked interest among human rights groups who have made it a point of contention. The Kumari is chosen from among a small number of girls who are between two and five years old, and it is asserted that their selection denies the young girls a normal life. The girls, during the selection process, are observed, examined, and tested. Certain traits are considered desirable and others not. To Allen this almost appears as a "Devi-beauty pageant".[10] In his introduction, he discusses the history of the Newar people, indigenous to the Kathmandu Valley, and provides a list of the 32 auspicious physical traits (*battis lakshana*s) of a Kumari.

The Kumaris are always selected from Newar Shakya families who are Buddhist by birth. Although there are several unsettled and unflattering folktales associated with Kumari being a Buddhist, embodying the form of a Hindu goddess in the body of a Buddhist girl is an important aspect of Nepali culture, mirrored in the admixture of Buddhist-Hindu worship. The cult of Kumari is thus an unambiguous example

2 The Kumari of Patan. Photograph: Akos Moskovits.

3 The Kumari of Patan in the courtyard of Hakhabaha on the occasion of the procession of lights (Mataya Jatra), two days after full moon in August (Shravanapurnima). The virgin goddess sits on a throne, flanked by two ceremonial sceptres. Her feet rest on a plate and a winnowing tablet, covered in offerings of biscuits and sweets. Photograph: N. Gutschow.

of Hindu-Buddhist amity and tolerance that has been observed for centuries. While Kumari was the source of power of the Nepali kings, she has also remained one of the most popular deities of ceremony across religious and ethnic divides.

The goddess herself, present in the living girl who is selected, is the Hindu goddess Taleju. She is the embodiment of Durga, the powerful mother-goddess who is prevalent in much historical literature and present-day worship. The girl, of course, is a virgin and is pre-pubescent. She must be removed from office at the first sign of menstruation or any large loss of blood or of illness. She is the embodiment of purity and power. In many cultures, not just Hindu, there is power in a young girl's virginity that symbolizes purity. Purity and power are often related, and we can here make a comparison with the Virgin Mary, the "mother" of God, who gave birth as a virgin and remains a potent source of spirituality among Christians.[11]

In Practice: The Worship of Kumari

As with much of Hindu worship, darshan, or *seeing* and *being seen,* is vital to this kind of worship. Many devotees will wait for hours or even days for a glimpse of the Kumari. Much

of the literature about the worship of the Kumari attempts to portray the mystery and power surrounding the young girl. The average Nepali sees nothing untoward or abusive about their devotion to the young living goddess. It is necessary at this stage to question whether "Western" conceptions of modernity should always be imposed on a traditional society.

Michael Allen's work is pervaded with the outsider perspective in judging the Nepali conception of Kumari. For him, the girl is stigmatized for life; she is set aside for the purpose of blessing others while being kept in a palace/prison; her developmental years are ignored. This would not happen in the United States or Canada or Germany.[12]

Today, in the name of modernity, some members of human rights groups and the newly-elected government propose that the Kumari tradition be abolished. Why she has become a pawn in the game of power in the country's new polity is an interesting issue. I will argue against abolishing the Kumari tradition from cultural, social, and economic perspectives. At this point I should state that I grew up in a brahman family in Nepal, was educated partly in India, and have now lived in the United States for over four decades.

Present Context

My interest in the subject was sparked by a BBC news report in 2006.[13] I was so agitated by the report that I wrote a letter to the *Kathmandu Post*, which published it the same week. Scott Berry, an American writer who had co-authored the book *From Goddess to Mortal* with Rashmila Shakya,[14] a former Royal Kumari, read my letter and emailed me a message supporting my position on the issue. The BBC further reported that a petition to the court to abolish the Kumari tradition had been filed in 2007 by a human rights group on the grounds of exploitation and psychological damage suffered by the girls selected as Kumaris. Chunda Bajracharya, a researcher on Newari culture, wrote to the BBC pointing out that the tradition has not affected the individual rights of the Kumaris, but has, in fact, elevated their status in society as "someone divine, someone who's above the rest".[15]

Nepal's Supreme Court ruled on August 18, 2008 that the Royal Kumari should be able to move around freely and should attend school. This is a fundamental change in the tradition which prohibited Royal Kumaris until now from attending public school. When Sajani Shakya, Kumari of Bhaktapur, was brought to the United States in 2008 by British filmmaker Ishbel Whitaker to promote her documentary on Kumari, it created a great deal of controversy resulting in the resignation of Sajani Shakya from her post as Kumari. Although the Supreme Court ruled in favour of the human rights group, giving freedom of movement to Kumaris, it was not clear whether leaving the country was part of that freedom as well.

The newly elected government of Nepal is of Maoist persuasion that believes, in principle, neither in organized religion nor in religious institutions. Maoist lawmaker and winner of the constituent assembly election, Janardan Sharma, declared, "All institutions associated with the royal family and feudalism will have to be changed. The Kumari is not an essential institution for the new Nepal."[16] The argument is that because the Kumari is intimately associated with the royal house of Nepal, her cult should be abolished along with the monarchy. But the Kumari is also a part of Nepal's history, culture, and religion. She is adulated by the proletariat as well. After all, the suppression of religion did not work in Soviet Russia and will likely fail in China as well, as ideally any sort of suppression should.

It is true that the girls selected to be Kumaris are separated from their families and are required to live in the Kumari Ghar until they complete their term. That these young girls who would otherwise be in school playing with their friends are now suddenly plucked out of a household and kept in a controlled environment may beg issues for discussion. However, we must weigh the benefits accorded to the young girls such as special care, veneration, security, and home schooling, which they otherwise might not receive. Let us not forget also that the parents are often allowed to live with the Kumari at the Kumari Ghar to avoid any emotional problems that she may experience.

Although she may have no freedom to go out to play or do chores like any normal girl of her age, she is kept sufficiently entertained in her residence by her caretakers. The human rights group has charged that the Kumaris have been exploited. But exactly how and by whom, it has failed to explain.

Such terms as "exploitation" and "psychological damage" are loaded terms. Have members of the group actually researched the situation of the Kumaris? Have they interviewed the Kumaris to see how they feel about this issue? What is the percentage of girls that do not marry after they leave the Kumari House? What is their state of mental health while they try to lead a normal life? Of course, it is equally necessary that these questions be answered by those of us who take a stand in support of continuing the tradition as well. If there is a preponderance of evidence to suggest that they indeed suffer emotional damage because of social confinement and the sacred role they play, then we need to find ways to prevent this from happening, and to rehabilitate former Kumaris by providing vocational training, jobs, and a retirement package so that they may be comfortable in their post-Kumari life. Abolishing the Kumari tradition is not the answer.[17]

From the book co-authored by former Royal Kumari Rashmila Shakya as well as from two recent documentaries

4 Ekanta Kumari Sajani Shakya of Bhaktapur. She travelled to the USA, and lost her title as a result. She was finally ritually reinstated on her return. Photograph: Caroline Martin.

5 Kumari Ghar, residence of the Royal Kumari, Kathmandu, built by King Jayaprakash Malla in 1757. Photograph: Katherine Anne Harper.

6 Kumari Ghar, residence of the Royal Kumari, Kathmandu. Photograph © Dinodia.

on Kumaris produced by Western filmmakers, there is not a shred of evidence to suggest that the former Kumaris exhibit any post-traumatic disorders. In open interviews, all former Kumaris, including the oldest surviving one (Hira Lal Shakya who was said to be 85 when the documentary was made in 2005), enjoyed their role as Kumari and never regretted it. From what I saw, they all felt empowered and special, even if only for a few years. If the Kumaris do not feel that they have been exploited, isn't the human rights group acting as Big Brother? An objective and in-depth study of the Kumari tradition is urgently called for.

Conclusion

Nepal has many social problems. Here are a few: (1) Girls are being sold into prostitution every day. (2) In some parts of the country, girls who are barely 13 years old are being married to much older men, and these girls tend to become pregnant at a young age, exposing them to birth complications and even death. (3) Most girls are not given the opportunity to get an education, and instead of attending school, many underage girls are forced to work. These are not practices essential to Nepali religious tradition. They – more than the perceived violation of the Kumaris' civil rights – require our immediate attention.

By doing away with age-old customs, we are treading the path to wiping out the culture of ancient origin that gives Nepal its distinct identity. Cultural identity is no less important than political identity. Researchers and tourists come to Nepal not because the country is industrially advanced with skyscrapers and bullet trains; they come because of its heritage, its culture, its discrete architecture and natural beauty. The Kumari is part of Nepal's cultural and religious heritage. Although she was traditionally associated with the throne, she does not have to go just because Nepal has voted to abolish the monarchy. The Kumari's blessings can be directed to any head of state – including a president, a chairperson – who may require them even more than a king or queen, judging by the political chaos that prevails. Kumari is the people's goddess.

Notes

1 Michael Allen, *The Cult of Kumari: Virgin Worship in Nepal* (Kathmandu: Institute of Nepal and Asian Studies, Tribhuvan University, 1975).
2 Michael Allen, "Kumari or 'Virgin' Worship in Kathmandu Valley", *Journal of the Indian Anthropological Society*, 32/3, 1997. pp. 207–21.
3 The core of this article is derived from my earlier article that appeared in Asianart.com, an online journal. See Deepak Shimkhada, "The Future of Nepal's 'Living' Goddess: Is Her Death Necessary", http://www.asianart.com/articles/kumari/3.html, September 10, 2008. Then in December 2008, Adam Pave, a PhD student at Claremont Graduate University's School of Religion, wrote a paper for the seminar course I taught at the university contextualizing the Kumari's history within Allen's research. My article here has profited from Pave's research on the subject, for which I appreciate. Opinions expressed by

7 The temple of Taleju dwarfs the other buildings in the Durbar Square. Its height is increased by the addition of several stepped tiers. Photograph: Katherine Anne Harper.

Pave come from his unpublished 2008 paper titled "Kumari: Nepal's Living Goddess, Her History and Her Future", which has been quoted at various places in this article.
4 Mary S. Slusser, *Nepal Mandala: A Cultural Study of the Kathmandu Valley* (Princeton, New Jersey: Princeton University Press, 1982), Vol. 1, p. 311.
5 Slusser, p. 312.
6 Ibid.
7 Pave 2008.
8 Shimkhada 2008.
9 See Pave 2008.
10 Allen 1996, p. 134, fn. 8.
11 Francis X. Clooney, SJ, *Divine Mother, Blessed Mother: Hindu Goddesses and the Virgin Mary* (New York: Oxford University Press, 2005), p. 17.
12 Pave 2008.
13 "Nepal 'goddess' inquiry ordered", by Surendra Phuyal, BBC news report, November 6, 2006.
14 Rashmila Shakya and Scott Berry, *From Goddess to Mortal: The True Life Story of a Former Royal Kumari* (Kathmandu: Vajra Publications, 2005).
15 As quoted in the BBC report by Surendra Phuyal, November 6, 2006.
16 Reported in http://www.thaindian.com/newsportal/uncategorized/kings-end-spells-doom-for-nepals-living-goddesses_10043878.html.
17 Shimkhada 2008.

Index

Contributors

Deepak Shimkhada earned his PhD from Claremont Graduate University and taught courses in Asian art history and Asian religions at other colleges and universities in California. Now retired from Claremont McKenna College, he teaches at Claremont Graduate University as an adjunct professor. He is the author of several edited volumes and numerous book chapters and journal papers. He co-edited *The Constant and Changing Faces of the Goddess: Goddess Traditions of Asia* (2009).

Niels Gutschow was educated as an architect, planner, and architectural historian at Darmstadt University, Germany, where he received his PhD in 1973 on Japanese cities. He is an internationally known expert of architectural history and an honorary professor at the South Asia Institute, Heidelberg University. He has been working in Nepal since 1970 and currently divides his time between two worlds – Bhaktapur, Nepal, and Abtsteinach, Germany.

Katharina Weiler is an art historian who studied at the Universities of Heidelberg, Germany and Bern, Switzerland. For her PhD dissertation on "The Neoclassical Residences of the Newars in Nepal", she did extensive research in Nepal's recent architectural history for which she was awarded a Mary S. Slusser Research Grant by the Kathmandu Valley Preservation Trust. As a postdoctoral research fellow, she currently supervises "Aspects of Authenticity in Architectural Heritage Conservation", a research project under the aegis of "Cluster of Excellence – Asia and Europe in a Global Context: Shifting Asymmetries in Cultural Flows" at Heidelberg University.

Julia A.B. Hegewald is Professor and Head, Department of Asian and Islamic Art History at the Institute for Oriental and Asian Studies (IOA), University of Bonn. She graduated from the School of Oriental and African Studies (SOAS), University of London, from where she also holds a PhD in the history of art and architecture of South Asia. In Nepal, she has participated in archaeological excavations (Patan, Pashupatinath, and Jharkot/Muktinath), researched architecture and city planning, and worked with contemporary painters.

Ian Alsop lived in Kathmandu from 1970 to 1988, where he eventually learned the Newari language and became a student of Nepali cultural history. From 1980 he was involved in a project to produce a classical Newari dictionary, which is presently available online at www. newari.net. He has written numerous articles on Nepali and Tibetan art and culture. He is also editor of an online journal, www.asianart.com, and Managing Director of a Nepali company, Websoft International, which produces and manages websites. He lives in Santa Fe, New Mexico (where he and his family run a gallery of Asian fine art, Peaceful Wind, and the associated gallery of Himalayan contemporary art, PWContemporary), and makes frequent journeys to Nepal and Tibet.

Dina Bangdel is a historian of South Asian and Himalayan art. Her research focuses on Newar Buddhist art and ritual as well as contemporary Nepali art. Her publications include *Circle of Bliss: Buddhist Meditational Art* (2003), *Pilgrimage and Faith: Buddhism, Christianity, and Islam* (2010), and *Newar Buddhist Architecture: Sacred Space and Iconography* (forthcoming). She is an Associate Professor of Art History at Virginia Commonwealth University in Richmond, Virginia.

Katherine Anne Harper is Professor and Chair of Art History at Loyola Marymount University in Los Angeles, where she has taught courses on various fields of Asian and Ancient studies. She has a PhD in South Asian art history from the University of California at Los Angeles and has published two books on South Asian art. In addition, she has published numerous articles on various regions of Asia, including one about a prominent Nepal painter in the exhibition catalogue *The Unspoken: An Exhibition of Painting by Madan Chitrakar* (Kathmandu 2008).

Ani Kasten has been working in the ceramics medium since 2000, beginning with an apprenticeship with British ceramist Rupert Spira. After a year in England, she travelled to Kathmandu where she spent four years as head of a project for developing stoneware technology for a community of artisan potters in the village of Thimi. Her training in England and the exotic working environment in Nepal have infused Ani's sculptural vessels with a combined aesthetic. She now has a permanent workspace at Gateway Art Center in Brentwood, Maryland.

Sangita Rayamajhi holds a PhD degree in literature. She teaches literature and women's studies at the Asian University for Women (AUW), Chittagong, Bangladesh that enrols students from 14 countries of Southeast and South Asia. After more than two decades of teaching in Nepal and the US and with a substantial number of publications on women and development, and advocating women's causes through her writings in newspapers and magazines, she now helps graduate women become skilled and innovative professionals, service-oriented leaders in business, government, and community organizations in their own countries.

Miranda Shaw received a BA in Asian Art History from Ohio State University and an MA and PhD in Buddhist Studies from Harvard University. Her extensive field research in India and Nepal has been funded by the Fulbright Foundation, National Endowment for the Humanities, and American Academy of Religion. Shaw is Associate Professor of Religion at the University of Richmond, Virginia and continues to pursue research on the art, writings, and practices of tantric Buddhism. She is the author of several books and articles.

Tim Ward lived in Asia for six years. He is the author of five books, including the bestseller *What the Buddha Never Taught* (about his time living in a Buddhist monastery in Thailand), a new 20th-anniversary "reincarnation" edition of which was published in 2010. As an international communications consultant for economic, environmental, and development organizations, Tim travels to Asia several times a year. He is involved with Maiti Nepal, which rescues girls from sexual trafficking, and Today's Youth Asia, a leadership organization dedicated to training Nepal's youth. He lives in Washington DC.